MY YEAR

_____

MY POWER PHRASE

_____
_____
_____
_____
_____

MY GOAL

_____
_____
_____
_____

Copyright

YOUR INNER DIALOGUE: What Were You Thinking?!
A workbook with journaling prompts and challenges to ditch the mental hamster wheel.

~ Know something new ~

Paperback Version

Photo by author: St Joseph, Michigan 2020.

KDP Publishing, Amazon
ISBN: 978-1-7365463-3-8

The information in this book is intended to be educational, self-reflective, and is not intended to replace mental health services, clinical judgment, clinical assessment, or treatment and may not be suitable for some. The user of this book assumes the risks as a result of using it. The confidentiality of what you enter in this book is entirely dependent on who you allow to have access to it.

Whether you find this book useful or not please provide feedback by taking a quick survey at:

https://DrVic.org/surveys/

"It's going to take as long as it's going to take." – Dr. Vic

Table of Contents

"You're always only one move away from starting something great." – Dr. Vic

Introduction

There's a journey I take every day in my work that no one else is privy to; other people's minds. While we tend to think that counseling is for people to overcome unique adversities caused by trauma or brain imbalance and pathology, there are practical areas that challenge all minds no matter who we are or what we've faced. What I've found is that once those areas are resolved burdens of the mind tend to lift as well. Although the process for that resolve can vary, some *"therapies"* work better for some situations than others, what we tell ourselves about experiences can be the biggest challenge. We overthink, spin, and get stuck. Additionally, the options for making sense of experiences today are virtually limitless and in my experience most of them are not helpful. To feel empowered and navigate life we must start with the practical side of living.

In a world that spins on information beyond what human kind has ever experienced I find that there is one necessary question we must ask in order to survive the overstimulation and saturation:

What is most helpful to think about?

According to research it takes less than four seconds for new information to penetrate and stick in our psyche outside of conscious awareness. However, lengthier exposure tends to do the opposite, we may scrutinize and reject it by filtering against what we already know and can consciously process. In one particular study the participants were exposed to an advertising banner at the top of a webpage while looking for unrelated information. Although, none of them realized they had seen it, a post survey revealed that their mind grabbed onto it and favored the product over other unknown ones even though it was fictitious. This is the *mere exposure effect* and the brain-child of Dr. Zajonc.

Now, as someone who was conscious for most of the 1970's and 80's I reflect on the concept through a lens of irony. During an era when there was no internet, social media, or Dr. Google we lived with some degree of fear over the possibility that we could be *"brain washed"* by subliminal messaging of advertising companies. If that was the case then, what does that mean now?

Today, the world evolves around that exact type of feared exposure effect as we scroll endlessly through unbelievable amounts of data during most of our daytime hours. According to surveys about stress, most adults check the news several times per day and reportedly experience heightened distress as a result of it. Not to mention the increase in adolescent self-harm by those grown on the internet. What this means is that we dispense and utilize energy by thinking without thinking and evidently, it's exhausting and troubling us by suggestive materials. As information gets stored outside of our conscious awareness it can ping pong on even greater fears if the searching and scrolling prompts the brain to serve up whatever it has been exposed to. We'd like to think we control it by technological preference settings, but research has demonstrated that it may not be true. We are exposed to more than we perceive of seeing or that reaches our cognitive awareness. Which is why we must, now more than ever, ask ourselves the "*helpful-ness*" question. However, it also leads to a specific question for you:

What have _you_ been thinking?

In my experience there is *feeling-thinking* and *cognitive-thinking*. For example, when a client says, "*it didn't feel right*". It begs to question, is that a feeling or a thought? Well, it's both. That statement involves a perception of an emotion that is translated into thought. If you've been feeling something and it's perceived cognitively, then it's a feeling-thought by contrast to logic and problem-solving that can pull strictly from cognitive knowledge structures. Yes, there are other technical ways to explain it, but I find this resonates more with clients than psychobabble.

Why does it matter? Because emotions and feelings have the power to fuel distress while mere knowledge does not necessarily have that same effect. It depends on how your mind has stored information and paired associations therein. If I say, "*faucet*" that's most likely not going to stir any emotional content for you because it's not attached to anything emotional in your life-experience-vault, but if I say "*mother*" that might have some unique associations with memories and experiences. Understanding what you are thinking about must begin by considering the practical things we all need in order to live life in an "*effective*" and healthy way.

No matter how fancy we try to get with our terminology and quoting complicated psychological concepts, if we don't cover the basics first, diagnostics are simply false positives. Sustainable change and impact relative to things that are set in the mind take time. There is simply no way around it unless you resort to medication or experience a trauma.

In this book I cover the top areas that help clients set a healthy baseline and find resolve and understanding. Here is a brief look at the topics:

1. **January ~ Goals**. Finding balance between your true "wants" and life demands.
2. **February ~ Stressors**. Understanding vulnerabilities and minding your stressors.
3. **March ~ Needs**. Establishing your baseline of needs and higher-order wants.
4. **April ~ Values**. Learning about what matters to you in various contexts.
5. **May ~ Beliefs & Motivation**. Discovering why you do what you do.
6. **June ~ Strengths**. Recognizing and leveraging that which makes you feel empowered.
7. **July ~ Self-Care**. Balancing life's demands with needs and values for wellbeing.
8. **August ~ Relationships**. Navigating daily relating for sense of community / belonging.
9. **September ~ Boundaries**. Allowing for physical, emotional, and psychological space.
10. **October ~ Patterns & Habits**. What were you thinking?! Knowing your hamster wheel and what you want to change.

11. **November ~ Time**. Mapping your time and making the most of it.
12. **December** ~ Mindfulness. Seeking out ways to be present while memories are made.
13. **Chapter 13 – Set Up For Success**. Set up rules, reminders, and resources for more effective control in the new year.

If you aren't understanding and questioning what you are thinking, feeling, and doing in these areas before consulting Dr. Google, it's quite possible that you're also not feeling in control of your life.

When I began writing this book, I had this vision of a parent shaking their head and pointing a finger at a child who supposedly did something wrong and saying, *"what were you thinking*?!"*. Isn't that how we spend our lives, judging, blaming, questioning and wondering what we did wrong to feel so badly and why things went so horribly wrong? Unfortunately, that is more useless information. We can't fix what happened, but we can understand and set a plan to move forward in a new direction, which is why as a counselor I inevitably always ask myself the same type of question I posed to you at the beginning of the introduction, *"what information may be most helpful for this person that they can use this week?"*.

While the answers vary in detail there is one principle that always remains the same: everyone wants to know what's going on and how to manage it. More and more I'm finding that people are tired of hearing about depression, anxiety, and other mental conditions. I refer to it as *"mental hype"*. As someone who is trained to diagnose psychiatric conditions and mental illness, I am a bit tired of it too. Rebranding it by calling it *"mental health"* is still essentially selling the same thing, *"there is something wrong with you and you need help!"*. It's as if we can fall prey to the wiles of mental dysfunction at any moment but the truth is that you have more control than you think and knowing what your feeling-thoughts have been exposed to requires getting back to the basics of what the brain and mind need in order to operate optimally.

What's the answer for you?

I don't know what will be most helpful for you, but *you do*. Any true expert will tell you that they cannot help you or "fix" anything relative to how you feel without your involvement. All we have as experts are some academic and experiential knowledge based on data built from comparisons, which had little input from you. Therefore, no matter what we think we know as experts it's useless without intermingling with your knowledge relative to your unique situation. This means that you hold the key to making expert information operative and helpful. The good news is that with the right prompts you can make gains in key life areas by journaling to discover some of the answers for yourself. That is the intent of this book because:

"A mind stretched by new experiences can never go back to old dimensions" ~ *Unknown*

That quote represents 99% of what I've experienced in journeying through other's minds. Once a person perceive or "*sees*" something new: a unique perspective, insight, or possibility, they can never "*unsee*" it. Sometimes we refer to it as having an epiphany or "*breakthrough*", the point is that the clients do that themselves, not the counselor. In that way there really is nothing magical about counseling. It forces you to slow down and unpack things to see the small movable pieces, or at least it should. If you spend enough time in reflection and processing and avoid consults with Dr. Google, you can set new dimension in your own life.

Just like talking, journaling is an external process that can reshape internal ones by engaging sensory inputs. I can't count the times that clients say, "*hearing myself say that out loud makes it seem totally different*". Taking things out of the internal neurological spin cycle is like seeing a movie in 3D. Although recycling is good in everyday living it may not be so good for the mind if the stuff it's spinning on is negative and outdated. It can skew the lens of what is going on presently and limit what you '*believe*' you *can* do. Additionally, while your brain knows billions of things, your mind can only retrieve and work with a limited number at a time. Introducing new variables by prompts and opening up different processing channels can help you see things you couldn't otherwise see.

This is all to say that there are a lot of important conversations happening in the world today but none as important as the one happening in your mind, it is the one voice you have control over. Yet listening, understanding, and changing it is not as clear-cut as some approaches make it out to be. Most of the "*thinking*" that we do is automated but not in the way you might think – it doesn't happen to you, at least not without your implicit or explicit permission as defined by your life experiences, beliefs, values, needs, and other life influences. No matter which learning style, personality type, or some intellectual category you fit into, or have been told you are, there is room for change. *You* can be that change. However, there are some limitations to be aware of.

"You can only do what you know"

Although, thoughts can *feel* random that is seldom true. The mind picks up on things outside of conscious awareness and filters it through existing knowledge structures, emotional and logical, how we recognize that and use it is up to us. On any given day or moment your thoughts are probably toggling between different states of thinking that involve:

- ☐ Pleasure-seeking
- ☐ Listening and managing emotions and feelings
- ☐ Fixing and changing

☐   Problem-solving

☐   Acquiring understanding

Knowledge is therefore never complete as it depends on environmental or internal cues. In the first book of this *Dialogue Book Series*, I shared my own life struggles with thoughts and events, as infantile and elementary as they may have seemed, I own that s**t. It was a part of my process to heal my inner child and find my voice. Admittedly it may also have been a bit of homage to the hundreds of clients I've worked with the last two decades. People who shared their mind and gave me the privilege to be a part of their healing journey.

In this book the focus is entirely on you to help you discover your own inner dialogue, examine what you know, leverage what works, and find new control through everyday experiences. If you're someone who likes to map things out and problem-solve, this journal provides ways to:

✔   Engage and reflect in deeper ad functional meaning-making of daily life experiences.

✔   Gain personal insight for achieving greater life satisfaction and balance.

✔   Make psychological research work for and with you, not compare or speak against you.

✔   Find authenticity in your inner voice.

✔   Transcend bias to experience yourself outside your family- and friend-lens; how they see you or who they *need* you to be.

✔   Access knowledge in your psyche that may be concealed by everyday stress and busy-ness.

✔   Remember what works and use it even during times of stress and distress.

✔   Be more strategic than reactive.

✔   Develop consistency in effort of thought and action. You're probably already doing things "*right*" but need a way to capture the process, know your indicators, and how to activate change.

✔   Find ways to override your defaults and go-to's.

✔   Think about what is helpful rather than hurtful.

In the midst of an online world my clinical experience continues to support the idea that with different information most people can do something different with their lives. Sustainable clinical gains require neurological change which takes time and effort just like healing a broken leg. Cells need to regenerate, reorganize, gain strength to restructure. In the same way we are empowered through functional information that we can use and apply. By leveraging what we know and making small changes in key life-areas repeatedly we can learn how to use what we know in a more effective way to meet our needs and improve our quality of life.

Copyright © 2021, V. Lännerholm, PsyD (ABD), LPCC, LPC, NCC

"You know more than you think"

There are of course things that can keep you from accessing what you know and render the best of information useless. It's easy for the mind to get caught up in daily distractions and demands and feel stress or even distress. While the mindfulness chapter can certainly help you identify effective ways to manage that within yourself, the book provides additional chapters to store your own discoveries for quick and easy reference as needed... This still leaves the question:

What is most helpful to think about?

Certainly not what your mind has been exposed to by social media, news, or Dr. Google. The most helpful thing you can do for your mind is to think practically about what you CAN do. To understand what you value and believe about your strengths and abilities in order to have a plan to achieve your goals. Sometimes that requires change in habits, boundaries, and motivations and other times it warrants taking action to manage time, meet needs, and reshape stress. Whether improving self-care, getting through the day, creating more supportive relationships, or getting a new job, this book captures key life-areas that can be the foundational reference for years to come. While your internal dialogue may have bullied and deceived you to believe that you're broken and need fixing, you have the power by unfiltered access to your mind to explore and discover practical ways towards real life change.

There are two versions of this book: an E-book that gives you access to the prompts, questions, and tools anywhere you have your kindle, or the app. Rather than turning to Dr. Google you can return to your personal journaling project for the week. The paperback allows you to actively engage in reflective processing in the privacy of your own home. There are four weeks of journaling prompts for each month of the year. While there are usually four months with five weeks in them, but they tend to change from year to year. Therefore, this book does not include them but many of the activities may stretch beyond a week which then will allow for some overlap.

Be as honest as you can be in your reflections. Before writing down your thoughts, take a moment to review all the prompts in each section to let them simmer over the week and filter through different circumstances. You can use a pencil to make temporary notes as thoughts pop up and you can paperclip pages where you make important discoveries or that you want to revisit. Remember, this book can serve you long into the future to remind yourself of what works best for you.

As always, thank you for letting me be a hitchhiker in your journey, if only through my words. I hope you will find this workbook helpful to live more intentionally and make life work for you!

Onwards and safe travels my friend!

January ~ Goals

"Sometimes the best goal is to find space to breathe and recharge." – Dr. Vic

Do we really need goals? Well, yes. And even if we think we don't have them, it's important to note that all behavior is goal directed whether by conscious intent, conditioned habit, or instinct. While it may seem like an obvious fact, research states that when we do have goals, we do better than when we don't. Why? Because the demands to achieve a goal is directly proportionate to the effort we put in. If we don't have a goal then we don't try as hard, or at all, because expectations lack alignment with something favorable and foreseeable, the *"what's the point"* phenomenon.

What is a goal? A goal is an ideal state, a target that requires understating of an aim. Goals can be primary, secondary, implicit, or explicit. They can serve different functions like solving a problem or to obtain a gain. They are functionally intertwined with motivation to help navigate discrepancies between an ideal and a present reality, whether we give up or keep press on. They are representative of needs, wants, values, and beliefs. For example, a basic need can be hunger that compels you to seek out food to reduce physical discomfort or seek sleep when you are tired. It can also be working harder at your job to increase the chance of getting a raise or keeping a to-do list or calendar to remember chores, events, or responsibilities.

Goals can also relate to wants and values to support implicit psychological and emotional needs like having a sense of belonging, fun, safety, or even to feel competent. If a situation, or life in general, feels out of control you may look for ways to gain control (an ideal state target) even if it's misdirected. For example, coping with challenges at work may spill over at home when you yell at the kids for nothing or are rude to the grocery clerk. That's not to say it's an excuse but understanding your ideals and how goals operate in your life can provide a state of resilience to protect against stressors and even save relationships.

In this chapter you'll explore general goals based on what you explicitly know that you want. Once you have sorted out your process of goal setting and achievement other chapters will provide opportunity to explore needs, values, beliefs, and motivation. Tasks this month are:

1. Figuring out what you want.
2. Exploring relevant goals and setting a plan.
3. Testing a goal and discovering your process.
4. Evaluating and recalibrating to refine your approach.

"Everything is subject to change and as far as it pertains to you, you can be that change, if only you believe". – Dr. Vic

Week 1 ~ What Do You Want?

There are no goals too big or too small. This is your life, you design it. For this week, take a moment each day to review the following prompts. Let them simmer and see what you come up with then be honest in writing down your thoughts. At the end of the week, you'll do a review and make a decision of what goal you'll be taking on. Although this week will walk you through the mapping of your smallest to biggest goals, this month is not so much about "achievement" or "success" as it is about identifying what works for you and developing your best strategy. There is a list of "*Goal Ideas*" at the end of this chapter based on areas from *Life Satisfaction*[1] domains and common counseling goals to help you think through what you want. You can write down your own version of goals in that list for future reference as well. Another option is to use questioning with yourself for each goal similar to what counselors use to imagine an outcome, such as:

    …   If a miracle happened overnight, what would tomorrow look like?

    …   If there was one day left to live, what would you focus on?

    …   If you were granted three wishes, what would they be?

    …   If it didn't cost anything, what would you do?

Goal 1 ~ Something I need to get done tomorrow is:

_____

_____

How long would it take to achieve it? _____ (*hours or minutes*)

Why is this important to me? _____

_____

Is it my idea (voluntary) or others demands (external expectations – real or perceived)?

_____

What are the main steps involved from start to finish (*thinking, feeling, or actions*)?

☐   _____

☐   _____

☐   _____

☐   _____

☐   _____

Resources / support / preparations needed:

_____

_____

_____

When could you start taking the first step (*date/time*)? _____

How much time can you set aside each week to work on it (*hour, day, weekends, evenings*)?

_____

Goal 2 – If I get one thing done this week it must be:

_____

_____

How long would it take to achieve it? _____ (days, *hours, or minutes*)

Why is this important to me? _____

_____

Is it my idea (voluntary) or others demands (external expectations – real or perceived)?

_____

What are the main steps involved from start to finish (*thinking, feeling, or actions*)?

- ☐ _____
- ☐ _____
- ☐ _____
- ☐ _____
- ☐ _____

Resources / support / preparations needed:

_____

_____

_____

When could you start taking the first step (*date/time*)? _____

How much time can you set aside each week to work on it (*hour, day, weekends, evenings*)?

_____

Goal 3 – The most important events/things to do this month are:

_____

_____

_____

_____

_____

Choose one: how long would it take to achieve it? _____(days, hours, or minutes)

Why are these important to me? _____

_____

_____

_____

_____

Is it my idea (voluntary) or others demands (external expectations – real or perceived)?

_____

What are the main steps involved from start to finish (*thinking, feeling, or actions*)?

☐ _____

☐ _____

☐ _____

☐ _____

☐ _____

Resources / support / preparations needed:

_____

_____

_____

When could you start taking the first step (*date/time*)? _____

How much time can you set aside each week to work on it (*hour, day, weekends, evenings)*?

_____

Goal 4 – Something I struggle doing/achieving but want to accomplish is:

_____

_____

How long would it take to achieve it? _____ (*hours, or minutes*)

Why is this important to me? _____

_____

Is it my idea (voluntary) or others demands (external expectations – real or perceived)?

_____

What are the main steps involved from start to finish (*thinking, feeling, or actions*)?

☐ _____

☐ _____
☐ _____
☐ _____
☐ _____

Resources / support / preparations needed:

_____
_____
_____

When could you start taking the first step (*date/time*)? _____

How much time can you set aside each week to work on it (*hour, day, weekends, evenings*)?

_____

Goal 5 – Something I've always dreamed of doing is:

_____
_____

How long would it take to achieve it? _____ (*days, hours, or minutes*)

Why is this important to me? _____

_____

Is it my idea (voluntary) or others demands (external expectations – real or perceived)?

_____

What are the main steps involved from start to finish (*thinking, feeling, or actions*)?

☐ _____
☐ _____
☐ _____
☐ _____
☐ _____

Resources / support / preparations needed:

_____
_____
_____

When could you start taking the first step (*date/time*)? _____

How much time can you set aside each week to work on it (*hour, day, weekends, evenings*)?

_____

To-Do List Items

List regular tasks in the table below that you *must* always remember and that require more than 30 minutes of your time. After completing the list consider whether others can take some of them on or if you can contract with someone to do them. For tasks that take less than 30 minutes, set up a routine each day where you allocate 30 minutes just for those minor responsibilities.

✓	To-Do	Delegate?

Annual chores like spring cleaning, car or home maintenance that you must remember:

☐ _____

☐ _____

☐ _____

☐ _____

☐ _____

☐ _____

☐ _____

Any other observations for this week?

Week 2 ~ Setting a Plan

Planning is necessary to move successfully towards a goal. Things that can trip you up on the way to achieving a goal are experiences of happenstance or adverse situations out of your control. It those occur chronically those can set the stage for conditioned beliefs like learned helplessness. The way to work around that is to set small achievable goals and retrain the brain one step at a time by small successes.

Three rules

There are three basic rules that can guide your planning:

1. The first rule of goal achievement is clarifying your goal and knowing *how* you will do it. This is largely a motivational and belief piece where you know the carrot you'll be chasing and can envision the race track. While you don't need to know all the steps up front, it does appear to be important to have a general idea, like a map of various stops on a trip. You did most of this work in the previous week. These also include your W's – the who, what, when, where type of resources you'll need access to use.

2. The second rule is to use the S.M.A.R.T. method to work out details of the main steps and set a tracking process of success. This involves knowing what it's going to take in terms of availability of time, effort, and resources. Time can be one of the biggest barriers to goal achievement. We overestimate or underestimate what it is going to take. Some of the estimation was done in the previous week. This week you'll elaborate on that by smaller steps.

3. The third rule is of course based on "*Murphy's Law*" which essentially states that if something can go wrong – it will... or rather *nothing is perfect*, so expect some challenges. Ensuring this rule is incorporated can help you adapt and keep moving forward. Part of navigating contingencies is the emotional and psychological hurdles you can face. This is a force that involves your level of determination and commitment. Are you all in or only if it's "easy"?

Over the next few days spend some time considering the prompts that follow to incorporate these rules into your planning process for current and future goal adventures.

My Goal

Out of the "wants" that you explored last week, which <u>one</u> are you choosing to focus on? *(Choose only one. You can return later to use the action planning template to repeat the process for other goals).*

Goal 1 – tomorrow (immediate) _____

Goal 2 – this week _____

Goal 3 – this month _____

Goal 4 – a challenge _____

Goal 5 – a dream goal (long-term) _____

To-Do List item _____

The S.M.A.R.T. Rule

Based on the general steps you identified for your selected goal in the first week of journaling, establish the main markers for your journey to achieve that goal and elaborate on the details in the grid below. This is similar to project management where one goal may have as many as twenty tasks.

Don't worry about the order of steps until you have created what you believe to be an exhaustive list. Afterwards you can number them based on which step precedes another. Rather than complete this in one sitting, take a few days to consider and research what may be involved if it's something that's unfamiliar to you.

The column for "W's" is to make note of needed resources and accessibility to them – the who, what, when, where etc. Be sure that each step integrates the S.M.A.R.T. rule by making it specific/small (*each step has enough detail to be operationally meaningful and useful*), measurable (*you have a way to track progress and know when it's complete*), attainable/achievable (*you believe it's possible and know what is needed*), relevant (*the step pertains to the mission of the goal*), and has a timeline (*expectation of how long it will take and when it should, can, and/or will occur*).

Order	Objective with task details to achieve selected goal	W's
	· Step_____ Tasks _____ _____ _____ Success looks like: _____	
	· Step_____ Tasks _____ _____ _____ Success looks like: _____	
	· Step_____ Tasks _____ _____ _____ Success looks like: _____	

Order	Objective with task details to achieve selected goal	W's
	· Step_____ Tasks _____ _____ _____ Success looks like: _____	
	· Step_____ Tasks _____ _____ _____ Success looks like: _____	
	· Step_____ Tasks _____ _____ _____ Success looks like: _____	
	· Step_____ Tasks _____ _____ _____ Success looks like: _____	

Got Time?

In any given day we can be pulled in dozens of directions, least notable of which are those we do by automation or necessity. As a part of the planning process, it is useful to do a quick inventory of "unavoidables". There is a complete daily/hourly *Time Chart* tool in the month of November, but for this exercise, you'll be listing the things you must do or currently do on a daily and weekly basis. This will help you identify how many hours you have available to do something new. As you consider things to add to the list don't discriminate or judge your thoughts. You'll be able to weed through it to prioritize and move

Got Time?	Frequency & Time Spent		Priority Type			Who?
Categories Tasks	Week Days (20)	Weekends (10 days)	Survival Needs	Wants	4 Others	Me / Shared
Grocery shopping		2	x			S
Work & commute / prep	9		x			M
Sleep	8	8	x			M
Meal prep & eating	2	2	x			M
Personal care, hygiene & Partner	2	1	x			M
Child time & care	1.5	2		x	x	M
Household chores						S
Pet care	1	1		x	x	
Car or home maintenance		1	x			M
Budget & bills		1	x			M
Friends		3	x	x	x	
Family / relatives				x	x	
Hobby		2		x		
TV time						
Internet time						
Holidays						
Totals	470	230			700	
	20 x total	10 x total	Monthly available hours: 720			

Copyright © 2021, V. Lännerholm, DrVic.org

things around once you've listed all you can think of. You can be detailed or categorical depending on how many things you come up with. The picture here shows a sample of a final list. The person who completed this found 20 extra hours in a month that equated to 1 hour a day and a half hour on weekend days. However, they had eliminated TV/Internet time to make room.

What will you need to change to make room? You can use the grid to make your own discoveries and write down preliminary observations about your current schedule and availability here:

_____
_____
_____
_____
_____
_____

Got Time?	Frequency & Time Spent		Priority Type			Who?
Categories / Tasks	Week Days (20)	Weekends (10 days)	Survival Needs	Wants	4 Others	Me / Shared
Totals						
	20 x total	10 x total	Monthly available hours: 720			

How many extra hours do you have in a day, weekend, or month? _____

Where can you make room or put things on temporary hold until your goal is completed?

_____

Are there tasks you share with others or that you can delegate? _____

_____

Any other observations? _____

_____

_____

Time Commitment

So, you've identified the time you can allocate or maybe moved somethings around in your schedule, what does that translate to in terms of your time commitment? Here is a way to incorporate that into your planning process:

To get _started_ I will set aside time on (*date/day & time*) _____

and spend _____ (*minutes/hours*) working on Step #_____ Task _____

_____

I will remind myself by _____

During that time, I will focus on completing the following part of the task _____

_____

_____

_____

_____

_____

Contingencies

Contingency planning is necessary to anticipate and navigate disruptors, interruptions, and even discouragement. Judging and thinking too far ahead can impair goal achievement before it begins, it's important to stay focused by one step and task at a time and remind yourself that everything else will fall into place at its proper time. Some basic contingency strategies include:

    a.   Saying "NO" to new things.
    b.   Setting specific task reminders.
    c.   Being careful what you tell yourself about progress.
    d.   Grieving disappointments and moving on.
    e.   Not sitting too long with a task.
    f.   Setting adequate transition time.

Possible or anticipated distractions include:

_____
_____
_____
_____
_____

My contingencies to stay focused will be:

- ☐ Let people know in advance that I've got plans
- ☐ Block it off on my calendar
- ☐ Put a "do not disturb" sign on my door
- ☐ Turn my phone off / mute notifications
- ☐ Say NO to new projects, events, or responsibilities.
- ☐ Have a visual cue to remind myself of the task/goal for that time
- ☐ If I go on vacation, I will revisit my goals and values in this book to get back to a routine
- ☐ _____
- ☐ _____
- ☐ _____
- ☐ _____
- ☐ _____

Are You "All In"?

After all that analysis and exploration, how do you feel about your goal? Are you all in or questioning whether you can do it or not? Rate your attitudes and beliefs about goal setting and achievement. All success comes from some degree of tension and striving this means that you must be more determined to meet your goal than to avoid the work to achieve it.

5 = All in! Ready to give it all I got!
4 = Hopeful and ready to give it a try.
3 = Skeptical but doing something is better than doing nothing.
2 = Indifferent, if it happens it happens.
1 = doing this because I have to.

Past Goals	Rate	Current Goal	Rate
I believed I could do it		I believe I can do it	
My level of commitment		My level of commitment	
My level of determination		My level of determination	

Week 3 ~ Test Run

So, you have decided on the goal you want to tackle, outlined how you will do it, resources needed, contingencies and strategies, decided on level of determination, and settled on a time commitment. The goal for this week is to do a test run by taking the first step(s) towards your goal. Whether your goal is to get up on time or launch your own business, take a moment at the end of the day to write down your observations what you did, didn't do, which of the W's were relevant, which contingencies worked, and/or what you may need to adjust in your planning process, thinking, or other effort.

Day 1

_____
_____
_____
_____
_____
_____
_____
_____

Day 2

_____
_____
_____
_____
_____
_____
_____
_____

Day 3

_____
_____
_____
_____
_____
_____
_____
_____

Day 4

_____
_____
_____
_____
_____
_____
_____

Day 5

_____
_____
_____
_____
_____
_____
_____

Day 6

_____
_____
_____
_____
_____
_____
_____

Day 7

_____
_____
_____
_____
_____
_____
_____

Week 4 ~ Evaluate & Recalibrate

Here are some reflective prompts to explore your month's experience of goal setting and achievement. The goal I chose was:

_____

The steps/tasks I completed successfully were:

_____
_____
_____
_____
_____

Were there steps/tasks that needed further details to make them operationally sound and easy to follow?

_____
_____
_____
_____
_____

What barriers did you experience and how did you navigate them?

_____
_____
_____
_____

How did your time planning and commitment work for you? What changes did you need to make in your calendar, overestimating/underestimating, and how can you apply that to future goals and tasks?

_____
_____
_____
_____
_____
_____

Were there additional resources, time, space, people, or information that would have helped and what can you do in the future to identify gaps before taking on a task?

_____
_____
_____
_____
_____

What strategies in your contingency planning were most useful?

_____
_____
_____
_____
_____

Where there thoughts or feelings that were problematic? If so, describe them and how you got through it or coped to keep moving forward towards your goal:

_____
_____
_____
_____
_____
_____
_____

What will you do differently in planning, configuring, and attempting your next goal?

_____
_____
_____
_____
_____

To stay motivated, what will you need to remember in order to achieve your next goal?

_____
_____
_____
_____
_____

Goal Taxonomy: Ideas & Tasks

Work & Education

- ☐ Explore different careers / change careers
- ☐ Research job opportunities / find new job
- ☐ Create / maintain resume
- ☐ Write cover letter
- ☐ Apply for job
- ☐ Return to school / sign up for classes
- ☐ Earn a degree
- ☐ Advance my skills by attending seminar, conference, lecture
- ☐ Get certified in my field of work
- ☐ Be recognized as an expert in my field
- ☐ Climb the ladder of success / advance to leadership or management
- ☐ Network on LinkedIn / social media
- ☐ Build my brand / expand services
- ☐ Create a professional website
- ☐ Start a side business / hustle
- ☐ Increase earnings
- ☐ Increase my performance / productivity / efficiency at work
- ☐ Be happier in my work
- ☐ Reduce work hours / work load
- ☐ Begin retirement / succession planning
- ☐ Other: _____
- ☐ Other: _____
- ☐ Other: _____
- ☐ Other: _____
- ☐ Other: _____

_____
_____
_____
_____
_____

Communication

- ☐ Improve listening skills to become a more mindful and active listener
- ☐ Overcome fear of public speaking
- ☐ Reducing profanity
- ☐ Manage emotions
- ☐ Improve written communication
- ☐ Be more positive and engaging
- ☐ Develop negotiation skills
- ☐ Be more persuasive
- ☐ Reduce misinterpretations and assumptions and ask for clarification
- ☐ Explore new ways to express myself verbally
- ☐ Increase vocabulary
- ☐ Learn verbal conflict management
- ☐ Develop conversational style
- ☐ Understand and interpret other's body language and facial expressions better
- ☐ Manage my body language and facial expression
- ☐ Other: _____
- ☐ Other: _____
- ☐ Other: _____
- ☐ Other: _____
- ☐ Other: _____

_____
_____
_____
_____
_____
_____
_____
_____
_____
_____
_____
_____
_____

Community

- ☐ Feel more connected
- ☐ Attend local event _____
- ☐ Volunteer locally
- ☐ Participate in _____
- ☐ Support / contribute to a cause (community clean up, walkathon, soup kitchen, neighborhood watch...)
- ☐ Become an advocate
- ☐ Other: _____
- ☐ Other: _____
- ☐ Other: _____
- ☐ Other: _____
- ☐ Other: _____

Entertainment & Fun

- ☐ Attend a sports event
- ☐ Set a weekly or monthly family night
- ☐ Call a friend to get together
- ☐ See a movie
- ☐ Create a fun fund and start saving money
- ☐ Plan a trip
- ☐ Request vacation
- ☐ Attend a concert
- ☐ Other: _____
- ☐ Other: _____
- ☐ Other: _____
- ☐ Other: _____
- ☐ Other: _____

_____
_____
_____
_____
_____
_____
_____
_____
_____
_____
_____
_____
_____
_____
_____
_____
_____
_____
_____
_____
_____

Finances

- ☐ Manage money better / apply the "third's rule": pay bills, save some, spend some
- ☐ Pay bills on time
- ☐ Establish mindful spending habits
- ☐ Budget groceries
- ☐ Live below my means but within my needs
- ☐ Choose one debt to tackle
- ☐ Reduce credit card use
- ☐ Pay off credit cards
- ☐ Pay off loan
- ☐ Other: _____
- ☐ Other: _____
- ☐ Other: _____
- ☐ Other: _____
- ☐ Other: _____

_____
_____
_____
_____
_____
_____
_____
_____
_____
_____
_____
_____
_____
_____
_____
_____
_____
_____
_____

House and Home

- ☐ Inventory my wants and needs
- ☐ Relocating
    - o Contact a lender for home purchase approval
    - o Packing / securing boxes or materials
    - o Monitor
    - o Getting quotes and scheduling movers
    - o Establish a plan to secure a home
    - o Pack up house to move
    - o Research relocation options
- ☐ Household management
    - o Seasonal / major cleaning
    - o Clean out the closet / garage or
    - o Daily dishes
    - o Vacuuming / sweeping / mopping
    - o Dusting
    - o Decluttering
- ☐ Other: _____
- ☐ Other: _____
- ☐ Other: _____
- ☐ Other: _____
- ☐ Other: _____

_____
_____
_____
_____
_____
_____
_____
_____
_____
_____
_____
_____
_____
_____

Relationships

- ☐ Expand my friend circle
- ☐ Work on my helping behaviors
- ☐ Improve my relationships
- ☐ Listen more
- ☐ Make time for _____
- ☐ Other: _____
- ☐ Other: _____
- ☐ Other: _____
- ☐ Other: _____
- ☐ Other: _____

_____
_____
_____
_____
_____
_____
_____
_____
_____
_____
_____
_____
_____
_____
_____
_____
_____
_____
_____
_____
_____
_____
_____
_____
_____
_____
_____

Self-Care & Health

☐ Sleep hygiene – wind down 30 minutes before bedtime

☐ Better sleep environment – cooler/darker room, no TV in bed

☐ Sleep regularity – get to bed/get up at the same time each day

☐ Seek out a PCP (primary care doc/general practitioner)

☐ Schedule doctor/dentist visit

☐ Nutrition / diet – eat more of _____

☐ Nutrition / diet – eat less of _____

☐ Increase water intake

☐ Exercise – walk, jog, strength-training, aerobics, Zumba, dance

☐ Meditation / yoga

☐ Do a "clean month" without substances/alcohol

☐ Practice safe intimacy

☐ Inventory my values, needs, and wants

☐ Schedule regular relaxation and self-care days

☐ Manage mental health / go to counseling for:

☐ To learn new life skills	☐ Someone to talk to/listen
☐ Learn coping skills	☐ Work on a relationship(s)
☐ Improve communication	☐ Self-development & growth
☐ Process historical trauma	☐ Navigate life changes/transitions
☐ Understand myself	☐ Help with decision-making or critical thinking skills
☐ Basic support for living life	
☐ Manage emotional challenges	☐ Mental Health Assessment
☐ Substances to cope/problem	☐ Need tools/techniques to manage mental health/disorder
☐ Life planning	
☐ Learn how to manage conflict	☐ Process grief/loss
☐ Feel happier	☐ Work on self-esteem and confidence
☐ Life coaching	☐ General worries or social anxiety
☐ Overcome public speaking fears	☐ Family planning

_____
_____
_____
_____
_____
_____
_____

Spirituality

- ☐ Seek local spiritual or faith-based support
- ☐ Increase prayer time
- ☐ Study / read or learn about a religion or spiritual practice
- ☐ Join a religious organization
- ☐ Attend gatherings
- ☐ Explore faith and religion
- ☐ Participate in organized religious traditions
- ☐ Other: _____
- ☐ Other: _____
- ☐ Other: _____
- ☐ Other: _____
- ☐ Other: _____

_____
_____
_____
_____
_____
_____
_____
_____
_____
_____
_____
_____
_____
_____
_____
_____
_____
_____
_____

"The more you have, the more you have to take care of.
Simplify." – Dr. Vic

February ~ Stressors

*"Stress takes your breath away,
make sure you are breathing." ~ Dr. Vic*

The reality of stress is something we tend to miss. Yes, we know stress is bad for us and that exercise and meditation *can* help. However, if you think you know all about stress, I challenge you to examine the contents in this chapter with extra scrutiny. For far too long we have thrown the word "*stress*" around to the point that it's become elevator music. *That* is a serious problem because it allows stress to be a silent killer and even a scapegoat that steals our control. There are in fact things we can do with stress other than fight with it or manage it, but it begins with *awareness*, something that has been virtually eliminated through desensitization.

What is stress and what can you do about it, *really*? In this chapter you'll have opportunity to investigate your own stress response by examining three primary forces: physical and internal, environmental, and psychological. Lastly, you'll configure your own plan of attack to level the playing field between demand and resources. The ultimate goal at the end of four weeks is that you have the tools necessary to:

1. Gain an intimate understanding and self-awareness about your vulnerabilities and resources to manage your stress response.

2. Differentiate between a stress-memory and current events.

3. Understand "triggers", defaults, and go-to's.

4. Reconfigure and engage in more effective appraisal relative to stress.

5. Design your own plan for addressing stress in your life and building resilience.

Before embarking on the first week of information and prompts, take a moment to consider how you define stress. Write down what comes to mind in a brief narrative, *stress to me means*:

_____
_____
_____
_____
_____

My experience with stress this week has been:

_____

_____

_____

_____

_____

_____

_____

_____

_____

Stress in my family typically looks like:

_____

_____

_____

_____

_____

_____

_____

_____

_____

Stress I feel right now, or on a regular basis is like:

_____

_____

_____

_____

_____

_____

_____

_____

_____

_____

_____

_____

Week 1 ~ How Does Stress Impact You?

It's easy to identify when we have been or are stressed by what we think about how we are feeling in any given moment. We even anticipate stress by events, situations, or people that we don't like or don't feel like we have control over. The stronger stress and dread the more it can serve as a reinforcement and affects you even when you aren't faced with them. The result of that can go one of two ways. If it's immediate it can produce severe ANS arousal like a panic attack. If it's chronic, it can become a vicious internal cycle like a habit of the mind that escalates to avoidance or background noise that undermines resilience in other parts of life where the body takes the hit through aches, pains, and unexplainable ailments. Stress impact is both physical and psychological.

Stress is NOT something that happens to you, and it is not a disease. It's a natural response to an uncertainty about whether demand will outweigh resources or not - physical, cognitive, and/or emotional resources. Although the sequence of events varies depending on which research or theory you consult, stress detection that results in emotional upset involves tension felt viscerally in the body and/or overthinking that involves cognitive processing of past, present, and future. All in an attempt to control a perceived demand – internal or external, or what early researchers referred to as the attempt to *maintain homeostasis*.

The Autonomic Nervous System (ANS)

Homeostasis is something that all organisms need in order to sustain life. Some people need peace and quiet while others operate better on the go. Stress is the process and experience of rebalancing when a compromise to that "normalcy" or safety is detected.

Stress is often associated with anxiety which is fairly accurate. Anxiety is merely a word to describe the cognitive experience of ANS activation. Which is not to say that the ANS isn't operative until there is an adverse event, it's operative in a different way. Activation, also referred to as ANS arousal, can be felt by heart palpitations, racing pulse, sweating, inability to think straight, feeling dizzy, tightness in the neck or chest, even the pang in the gut when you realize something doesn't' feel right. The ANS controls everything from blood pressure and oxygen to the brain to all major organs and systems in the body. Which is why the sensation of ANS arousal can vary between people. Some even develop an adaptive mechanism to control it as in the case of chronic stress which may result in not feeling anything physically until after the threat is gone – "*unexplainable*" exhaustion, drain, or emotional upset when it is safe to finally "*let it all out*".

Recognizing how "*stress*" feels in *your* body and mind is critical to awareness of stress in your life and thus managing it more effectively. To begin, review the chart provided here and identify some of the ways you feel stress physically.

Symptoms Worksheet

Physical System Impact	My Symptoms and Mind Impact
Digestion (appetite, cramping, fullness, bloating, nausea)	
Blood flow (pressure, heart rate, constriction, visual, cognitions, sexual changes)	
Immune system (under-overactive, allergies)	
Oxygen levels (breathing, compromised cognitive processing and memory recall function)	
Muscle control (contraction, tension, movements, speech, shaking, spasms)	
Body temperature (hot, cold)	
Metabolism (weight loss/gain)	
Body fluids (sweat, tears etc.)	
Liver, kidneys (urination / defecation changes, glucose)	
Other/Endocrine (menstrual cycle, epinephrine, thyroid, adrenals, hormones)	
Circadian Rhythm changes (sleep etc.)	
Neurotransmitters and hormones (extreme emotional highs/lows)	

*** This chart was compiled by the functions/organs listed here have much crossover and may not be an exact categorization. Consult with your primary care physician to discuss any specific concerns you have about your physical functioning.

Any other observations?

_____
_____
_____
_____
_____

Week 2 ~ Stress Inventory

While we tend to think we feel stressed because of situations or events around us, and it may be true in a way, those are mere vulnerabilities that we respond to in healthy or unhealthy ways. There are ways to redefine interpretive responses to stressors through appraisal as long as you know what to look for and what to do when you make a discovery. In other words, instead of letting your physiological system operate mindlessly to manage a preferred homeostatic state you take conscious control to recognize when you are approaching your limit.

While it is true that you can redefine limits, as Dr. Robertson outlined in his book *"The Stress Test"* (which I highly recommend by the way) the process of adaption, extinction of a defined perimeter of beliefs and responses, or extending your boundaries, can take time. You must decide what your level of effort will be similar to the process you defined in goal setting and achievement to find success. There will be more on that in other chapters.

Since it's official formulation and entry in the 1950's, "stress" has been a race we've tried to outrun. We exercise, yoga, meditate, and try to be mindful but there is no "cure". There has been much research around stress. In 1967 Holmes and Rahe developed a *"Social Readjustment Rating Scale (SRRS)"* which has since evolved into a variety of stress indexes. The original intent of the SRRS was to explore the impact of stress on health. As with other notable stress research, all have discovered the same thing; indeed, stress compromises physiological and psychological wellbeing.

For this week, let the items in the table below simmer through your mind for a few days and filter through a few questions. Then fill in the empty fields with examples and your own notes for easy reference later. Be sure to mark whether it's recurrent (happening PRESENTLY) or historical (happened in the PAST) stressor:

☐ When I think of/experience this does it cause me distress/stress?

☐ Are there situations that bring up similar feelings?

☐ Do I feel different now than when it happened in the past?

*** *Caution: some of these may bring up difficult memories for you, if you have concerns about that be sure to contact a mental health counselor to process it with. The national help line is 1-800-662-HELP (4357) or for a crisis call 1-800-273-8255 (online chat available).*

#	Stressor	Provide an Example	R-ecurrent H-istorical
1.	Loss/Grief, Death		
2.	Separation or Divorce		
3.	Relationship Conflict		
4.	Intimacy Challenges		
5.	Legal Issues or Jail		
6.	Work or School Problems		

#	Stressor	Provide an Example	R-ecurrent H-istorical
7.	Peer Pressure		
8.	Caregiving Adult or Child		
9.	Safety (Home/Work)		
10.	Economic / Financial		
11.	Childhood Adversity or Trauma		
12.	Physical Health Conditions		
13.	Role / Life Confusion		
14.	Career / Job Change or Retirement		
15.	Youth to Adult Transition		
16.	Trauma or Injury		
17.	Military Experiences or War		
18.	Cultural or Social Injustice		
19.	Religion / Spirituality		
20.	Daily Routine Disruption		
21.	Daily Responsibilities		
22.	Food or Eating		
23.	Things & Ownership		
24.	Shopping		
25.	Transportation, Traffic		
26.	Social Media, Internet Searching		
27.	Online Gaming or Gambling		
28.	Bad Habit or Substance Abuse Alcohol/Addiction		
29.	Relocation / Moving		
30.	Holiday / Vacation Demands		
31.	Achievement or Success		
32.	Basics (shelter, sleep, nutrition, safety…)		
33.	Transitions (between tasks or events)		
34.	Self-Demand (to-do lists)		
35.	Unexpected / Unplanned Events or Demands		
36.	Other:		
37.	Other:		
38.	Other:		

Week 3 ~ Triggers

There are three things we must understand to move successfully into the future: where we've been, where we are, and where we're headed. The trick is to not get them mixed up because the mind can't tell time and what happened ten years ago can feel the same today. Yet you only have today to:

- ☐ Reconfigure and make sense of what didn't work yesterday;
- ☐ Set a plan for giving it another try or doing something different tomorrow;
- ☐ And make sure to refuel today before setting sail again into the future.

Unfortunately, we can only do what we know which means the past can serve as a lens that skews beliefs and anticipations about tomorrow so to drain whatever energy we have today. The key is to manage that by recognizing and redefining the most common issues in navigating daily living, specifically *"triggers"*. While *"triggers"* have received a bad rap, they are a necessary evil in the ways that the mind and memory work. They are nothing more than *cues* and *primers* that allow the mind to access information in memories to make sense of current events. They determine if there is a threat to homeostasis by flushing through old emotions, feelings, experiences, thoughts, habits, beliefs, and so on. While they can make things *"feel"* real in the moment, they are operating on your historical information rather than a true reality.

Over the next few days take some time to reflect on your experiences and potential similarities with your historical context. Use the stress inventory and your ANS activation discoveries to recognize where things come from for you and what your relative *"triggers/cues"* may look like. The goal is to obtain objectivity rather than engage with the memory as if it's happening now, which is what we tend to do. Use the prompts below like watching a movie of events unfolding in a story. You are the observer describing them and telling it rather than an actor therein. In this first entry consider what your mind/body uses to activate difficult thoughts or feelings through thought, sight, sound, or smell etc.:

My *negative* triggers are:

- ☐ _____
- ☐ _____
- ☐ _____
- ☐ _____
- ☐ _____
- ☐ _____
- ☐ _____

Any other observations?

_____

_____

_____

_____

_____

_____

_____

_____

_____

_____

The notion that we should mind our mental health by blocking, tuning out, or avoiding "*triggers*" can actually backfire terribly and is not advisable from a purely psychologically functional perspective. Avoidance only reinforces the problem and if associated with a trauma or adversity can generalize perceptions to the point where *harmless* information is interpreted as *harmful*. The only way to deal effectively with triggers is to understand the root cause, work with a professional to yank them out, establish differentiation between now and the past, and grow a healthy coping mechanism and perception in its place. Once you do so, it will cause your internal physiological and psychological system to stop seeing it as a threat to homeostasis and therefore no longer react aggressively to cause an emotional disturbance. While it sounds simple in some instances like trauma it may not be and does require professional guidance to work through.

Triggers you have been using for *avoidance* include:

☐ _____

☐ _____

☐ _____

☐ _____

☐ _____

☐ _____

☐ _____

Any other observations?

_____

_____

_____

_____

_____

Triggers can also work in other ways, like the smell of baking cookies and fond childhood memories or seeing a picture of a loved one and feeling that flutter inside. That's why we see so much hype around positive psychology, that stuff really works to improve a sense of wellbeing just as well as the negative works to deplete it. It's up to you to choose what to focus on and which to neutralize rather than avoid. Unfortunately, if the authority of triggers has been sustained for any length of time and developed a deep neurological rut, or if you have ones that have been subconsciously operative, then it may require more complex interventions. However, a simplified layout of that change process involves intentional differentiation and recognizing what is a memory-experience versus a current threat to turn triggers into useful memory tools that make you feel better rather than bad. What are some things that when they come to mind serve you in recalling fond memories or feel good at the sight of them? What warms your heart?

My *positive* triggers are:

☐ _____
☐ _____
☐ _____
☐ _____
☐ _____

Any other observations?

_____
_____
_____
_____
_____

Stress and Distress Complications

More than a billion things exist in your mind relative to your entire life of exposure to information and experiences, but you can only access a handful of them at any given time. Whether it is remembering what to pick up at the store, to check your to-do list, or set an alarm to get up in the morning, stress and distress can divert from paying attention and having access to what is stored in your brain. This is also why some self-help tests for anxiety and depression use "*forgetfulness*" as a criterion. Neurologically the brain's cognitive functioning tends to be impaired during times of high ANS activation. Why? The body/mind are busy tending to a perceived "*threat*"! You, trying to remember where you put your keys can be relatively miniscule in comparison.

This doesn't mean you have an anxiety or depression disorder, but it should serve as a red flag that your mind and body are struggling to maintain homeostasis. Much of regaining your control then is dependent on what you do and how you respond. The bottom line is that when you are stressed whatever great work you do in this journaling workbook may fall outside of your cognitive wherewithal at any given moment. Finding ways to recognize when you are hitting a maxed-out state and what the path to it looks like can help you set a plan for intervention before you hit a breaking point.

How many stressors does it take before you feel like you're about to lose it? Consider the ones in your inventory and envision a recent day where things got out of control, or you reached a melt-down. Describe it and recognize which stressor put you over the edge.

_____
_____
_____
_____
_____
_____
_____
_____
_____
_____
_____
_____
_____
_____
_____
_____

What if the stressors had occurred in a different order, would that have made a difference?

_____
_____
_____
_____
_____
_____
_____
_____
_____
_____

Week 4 ~ Plan of Resilience

This month you have spent time identifying and understanding how stress impacts you. You covered three realms of stress that can contribute to an internal destabilized and distressed state: your internal physical response, environmental cues, and historical information that fuel cognitive and emotional processing. This week you'll be setting the parameters for appraising your stress response when it does occur and setting a plan to avoid the rabbit holes to begin with. Key tasks:

☐ Identify indicators and vulnerabilities
☐ Identify resilience factors and what works

Physical Indicators

List your most important signals that may indicate that your ANS is activated – how will you know when your mind/body is interpreting something as a threat and escalating into stress?

_____
_____
_____
_____
_____
_____
_____
_____
_____
_____

Environmental Cues

List the most prominent events/experiences that have potential to activate a stress response – how will you know when your mind is assessing a potential threat (thoughts/feelings/emotions)?

_____
_____
_____
_____
_____
_____
_____

_____

_____

_____

_____

_____

_____

Historical Information

List the most common emotional experiences you have in the present that seem to be linked to, or feel similar, to your past that tend to activate your ANS presently – how will you differentiate between now and then "emotions"?

_____

_____

_____

_____

_____

_____

_____

_____

_____

_____

_____

_____

Stress Operations & Vulnerabilities

Understanding and using what you know during times of stress can feel impossible. It's critical to have a plan in advance of any stressor. For example, if you want to use deep breathing techniques or mindfulness, don't wait until you have a stress response to practice them. Practice the techniques and make them a habit in the mind daily so it is easily accessible as a default in your brain when you need it.

Now, that you've taken the time to gain more self-awareness of how stress manifests in your body and what some of the cues are it's time to set a plan that works for you. Just like the goal planning process you'll want to decide where the boundaries lie, resource, you'll need, and how to remind yourself what works to maintain homeostasis or at least avoid a melt-down. The best question you can ask yourself every morning is:

"How many stressors are already at play?".

For example, if you have a physical injury or chronic condition that can count as 1. If you then also had an argument with a coworker and you have to face the music in a couple of hours, that makes 2. If you get to your kitchen and the dog peed on the floor, that makes 3. The kids won't get ready in time? 4... and so on. While that may seem like a morning to ruin all mornings, even the rest of the day, you *can* set a plan to not let it get to you or a plan to not add to it if you recognize what is going on more than you churn on how *"awful"* it is. Knowing it's temporary and not permanent can help your mind navigate it. However, you must recognize when you are about to enter a high-risk zone, your thresholds of tolerance and coping boundaries.

Thresholds & High-Risk Zones

Where are your thresholds? Being able to *"brush things off"* is not necessarily a coping mechanism and can send adversities underground only to wreak havoc if one more thing happens. Make a note of what you should look for in yourself, this will be one of your internal red flags to begin paying attention and work through it.

I can usually overlook *or "brush off"* the following:

_____
_____
_____
_____
_____

While we like to find the *"one thing"* to blame, it's often not one thing at all but rather a compounding effect of several over a period of time, and within close proximity. Reflect on your observations the past few weeks, is there anything that stands out to help you calculate how many things that may be or specific things that hold more weight than others to put you over the edge?

When I hit #_____ of issues in a day / week or if it has to do with _____
_____
_____
_____
_____
_____

that is the last straw.

Here are some other areas that are standard points of vulnerability that undermine resilience for the body / mind – you can add your own to this list from your notes for easy reference as well:

- ✓ Physical / chronic conditions (injury, illness, pain, headache, hunger)
- ✓ Discord and disagreements
- ✓ Frustrated goals
- ✓ Hormone or neurotransmitter shifts (cortisol, adrenaline, dopamine, reproductive hormones)
- ✓ _____
- ✓ _____
- ✓ _____

- ✓ Alcohol and other substances during use and afterwards for days
- ✓ Running / being late
- ✓ Uncertainty / unsafe conditions
- ✓ Unresolved problems
- ✓ Extremes of weather (heat, cold, wind)
- ✓ _____
- ✓ _____
- ✓ _____

Thresholds aren't just relevant in terms of how often or how many, but also their timing. Here are some things you may want to keep in mind for your own monitoring and planning.

My *most* stressful days of the week are (write the day and your reasons):

_____
_____
_____
_____
_____

My *most* stressful times of the year (write the month/holiday and reason):

_____
_____
_____
_____
_____

When you recognize any of the above it may be important to ask yourself, "*what does it mean*"? Is there truly impending doom or is it a memory? Take a moment to reflect on what you wrote and whether it relates to thoughts or events and timing thereof?

_____
_____
_____

_____
_____
_____
_____
_____
_____
_____
_____
_____
_____
_____
_____
_____
_____
_____
_____
_____
_____

Resilience Plan

What can you do differently to manage stress and distress? Here are some prompts to think it through.

In order to manage my stress, I need to start my day:
(List things like thinking, doing, reminding myself, avoiding...)

_____
_____
_____
_____
_____

When I start to feel or think _____
I know it's time to _____
_____
_____
_____

My daily high-risk zones are:

_____
_____
_____
_____
_____

It can take anywhere from 30 minutes to an hour <u>after</u> a "*threat*" is removed (real or perceived) before the ANS begins to return to normal functioning. The reason is simple; physical systems need to restore order in levels of oxygen, blood flow, hormones and to restart normal functions like digestion and immune protective processes. It's like rebooting your phone or laptop after it freezes up from too many apps or processes running all at once. This means that after you "*feel*" the pressure lift it's time for recovery. How you do that and how you make sense of distress and stress usually depends on whether you believe it can happen randomly or that you can predict it.

Take some time to reflect on what you believe about your experience and make a decision about what to look for next time, what you'll believe, and how you can make it more manageable or avoidable.

_____

_____

_____

_____

_____

_____

_____

_____

_____

_____

_____

_____

_____

_____

_____

There are a wealth of resources from researchers and experts in the field of stress that can help you, but it may take some time to actively seek out solutions that fit your lifestyle and experiences. If one doesn't work it doesn't mean that *nothing* works for you or that there is something wrong, it just means you need to keep searching.

Tools and techniques that help me de-stress:

_____

_____

_____

_____

_____

_____

Here are some common tricks that can work in concert with the standard ones mentioned earlier. You can add your own as well for easy reference and reminders later:

✓ Tend to the basics: physical health and wellbeing

✓ Set a time/reach out to settle disputes

✓ Recalibrate goals and break down tasks to more manageable steps

✓ Find time to decompress after a difficult event/experience – minimum 1 hour

✓ Revisit your positive triggers and use them to redirect

✓ Plan ahead and make sure you incorporate weather variables if applicable

✓ Say NO, as needed and without judgment.

✓ Avoid alcohol and other substances that impact ANS activity

✓ Give yourself transition and prep time before and between events/tasks

✓ Focus on what you CAN do

✓ Set a plan to tackle a problem instead of allowing your mind to spin on it. Set a day, time, and find someone to work with you on it

✓ _____

✓ _____

✓ _____

✓ _____

✓ _____

Any other observations of what works for you?

_____

_____

_____

When To Seek Professional Guidance

If you find that your stress or distress is unmanageable, unbearable, or you feel overwhelmed a lot, it may be time to seek out someone who can help you process it objectively. If nothing you have tried works and you feel despair surfacing that's usually a good point to find a professional counselor or psychologist to check in with. This doesn't mean you have a mental disorder... no matter how bad it _feels_! All knowledge is incomplete, and stress is one of those brain influences that we've been so desensitized to that we believe we should be able to handle it and if we don't, we're somehow not smart or tough enough, or there is something seriously wrong and unfortunately Dr. Google is all too ready and willing to confirm it.

Stress can blind us to solutions even if our brain knows them. That knowledge gets buried under activation of other neurological pathways intended for survival. Having someone who is not clouded by those emotional channels to help dig into the logical and manageable ones can get you back on track. The real danger is getting to a point of believing that you are "ill", so catch yourself before you go there and get the distress/stress resolved.

"You can only do what you can do." – M.P.

March ~ Needs

*"Tired? Get some rest, sleep, or recharge.
It doesn't have to be complicated.
Know your needs, meet your needs." ~ Dr. Vic*

How often do you consider your own needs? What are *"needs"* anyway? Defining needs can be a matter of theory and individual preference. Different theories and models over time have defined human *"needs"* in different ways from psychodynamic, cognitive, behavioral, to humanistic, existential, and neurobiological perspectives. However, when it comes to daily application of understanding and meeting *your* needs, it ultimately comes down to what you decide to believe about them. There are effective and ineffective ways to think about needs and in this chapter, you'll have opportunity to define what that means for you.

From the minute we're born we have needs and try to meet them by instinct until our communication evolves into language and words. The default dialogue that plays in most minds as adults are what was recorded during childhood or other lengthy life experiences based on feedback from others like family or friends. The dynamics of those interactions and experiences undoubtedly created implicit rules or messages that you may still follow unknowingly. Some may have involved guilting, dismissing, invalidating, or embarrassment to create ineffective and negative beliefs or expressions for you today. The most common ones associated with *"need"* include:

- Being Needy
- Demanding
- High maintenance
- Fussy
- Unreasonable
- Talking back
- Undeserving
- A drama queen
- Weak
- Selfish

However, needs are multifaceted and necessary indicators for living life and maintaining homeostasis. Unfortunately, once age 18 rolls around those old messages tend to be heavily integrated into our psyche and may continue to play regardless of the presence of parents, family, or friends who planted them. The responsibility for meeting our needs then become our own and if we haven't been shown how to pay attention to them in a healthy way we may continue to operate from a fear-base and dismiss, invalidate, or minimize ourselves. Figuring out which is which to set a new strategy for meeting them may require a bit of a remodel.

The tasks and outcomes for this chapter will guide you in:

1. Examining your own baseline of needs.

2. Identifying higher-order and primary needs and wants towards greater life satisfaction.

3. Establish a regular inventory of check-ins with yourself.

4. Setting an overall plan of strategies to use in meeting your needs; new rules and new "shoulds".

How do you currently define your needs?

_____
_____
_____
_____
_____
_____
_____
_____
_____
_____
_____
_____
_____
_____
_____
_____
_____
_____
_____
_____
_____
_____
_____
_____

Week 1 ~ Your Baseline

So, where did *your* needs come from? With this week's journal prompts you'll be doing some excavating to identify and define your baseline. As with other exercises, be honest and give your mind opportunity to dig through its network of memories and information by letting time pass between when you read the prompts and respond. Letting information simmer throughout a day can give new perspective and insight as you pass through experiences and navigate environmental cues.

All humans have the same basic needs physically. The body needs nutrition to fuel energy, growth, and healing. It also needs movement and exercise to maintain mobility and flexibility as well as gain and maintain strength and resilience within the cardiovascular, immune, the nervous system, and other operations. This is the very basic of survival needs for homeostasis.

Those physical systems are of course interconnected with psychological basic needs. If you are stressed about whether you'll have a place to live or not the body reacts in response to the cognitive and emotional signals. It does so by redirecting system functions from normal operations to releasing hormones that can harm the body if they are experienced chronically. Therefore, psychological needs of security and certainty, i.e. knowing where you'll lay your head at night and what you'll eat, are critically important by comparison to whether you'll win the lottery or get the car you want or not.

The focus this week is on the very barebone basics of your baseline and next week you'll tackle the higher-order needs in terms of *"wants"*.

The Basics

The table on the next page lists some core needs that are commonly referenced by *Choice Theory Psychology* and are used in *Humanistic Psychology – Maslow's Hierarchy*. In this exercise give each category some thought then rate them from #1 (*most important*) to #5 (*least important*). You'll revisit these later in the chapters on *Self-Care* and *Relationships*.

Think of these as the bare minimum you need in order to feel *"OK"* or *"normal"*. Be sure to write down examples for each of them before rating them. For example, you may define *"shelter"* in *"Basic Survival"* as living in a house rather than an apartment. If so, make a note of your reasoning for that need. *What is it about a house versus an apartment that meets your needs?* Maybe you have pets or a garden that can't be maintained otherwise.

If you feel creative, you may even want to get a small poster board and pull together visual representations like photographs or drawings into a *"needs vision board"*.

Basic Needs Inventory

Basic Survival *(safety, food, water, shelter, health etc.)*

Belonging *(love, relatedness, acceptance, caring, culture, language, tradition, identity etc.)*

Fun *(discovery, learning, adventure, exploring, enjoyment etc.)*

Power *(competence, meaning, achievement, importance, control etc.)*

Freedom & Autonomy *(choice, expression of thought/voice, flexibility, creativity etc.)*

Adapted from Dr. William Glasser, 1998, Choice Theory Psychology

Where'd They Come From?

Understanding your baseline to determine importance of your needs and whether some of them are outdated may require some reflection on how needs were expressed and met in your family. For example, *how did you and your siblings get your way with each other or withing the family unit*? Asking, crying, pity, yelling, hitting, avoiding, guilting, silent treatment or some other way?

_____
_____
_____
_____
_____
_____
_____
_____

When your mom needed you to do something, what did she say or do?

_____
_____
_____
_____
_____
_____
_____

When your dad needed you to do something, what did he say or do?

_____
_____
_____
_____
_____
_____
_____

How did your parents communicate needs with each other? What did they do or say to get each other to do what they wanted (mowing the yard, cleaning, cooking, paying bills, shopping etc.)?

_____
_____
_____
_____
_____

How do you and your partner express and communicate your needs with each other now, or what does that look like in your relationship with your kids?

_____

_____

_____

_____

_____

_____

_____

Is the value of any of your needs determined by others and under which circumstances are your needs ok or not ok?

_____

_____

_____

_____

_____

_____

_____

What do you believe about your "*needs*"?

_____

_____

_____

_____

_____

_____

Any other observations about your needs?

_____

_____

_____

_____

_____

_____

_____

_____

_____

Week 2 ~ Higher-Order Needs: Wants

Last week you explored the origin of your basic needs and what your baseline may be. This week you'll be able to expand on that baseline to consider what you *want* in the context of life satisfaction. For this exercise you may want to revisit your notes in the chapter on Goals where you identified key areas of "*wants*". While needs aren't the same as wants, meeting your needs requires that you honor and fulfil those areas as well.

According to research people tend to be more inclined to take care of themselves (mind/body) when higher-order desires are met (yes, it contradicts Maslow's work slightly). What that does support is that homeostasis is truly about balance as a whole. We need a little of both types; to eat nutritional meals, sleep, and exercise just as much as we need to do things that we enjoy like going to the movies, hanging out with friends, or eating a treat.

Too often we focus on keeping the body alive while ignoring the real heart of the matter which is living. To meet both physiological and psychological needs that then generate what is often referenced as life satisfaction or wellbeing. Popular models for wellness involve several dimensions: social, emotional, spiritual, occupational, financial, environmental, physical, and intellectual. Some of those dimensions will be incorporated into the next few chapters beginning with the life satisfaction model.

Life Satisfaction

There is a wealth of research on how to define life satisfaction and quality of life. Various surveys, tools, and questionnaires. Some even target specific populations or life situations. This section provides a brief set of statements to help you think about *your* dimensions of satisfaction. Review the table on the next page and answer the prompts. If you find that you don't answer "YES" to as many as you would like it may be time to ask another question: *What will it take to bring the score up for you?* Maybe you answered "YES" to 3 out of 10. *What would need to change to make it 5 out of 10? What would 2 points represent for you?*

As with other tools of reflection in this journal, take your time and use each day of the week to make new observations for each question. You may even discover new goals you'd like to set for yourself or needs you had not thought of. You can then return to those sections of your journal to set reminders or make a note of it. When considering the prompts in the table on the next page it is important that you define the variables that could contribute to making each of the statements a reality for you in order to use them for your goals.

For those things that you answer "NO" to, try to think of at least 3 things that would change your answer to "YES". As with other tools in this book, this is an exploratory piece for self-discovery and growth, there are no "*scores*" or diagnostics. These are for you to use to make the changes you want to make and work towards making life work for you.

Life Satisfaction Inventory

	Statement of Satisfaction	Yes?	No? (Enter key points from your reflection)
1	My life is better than most.		Compared to whom? - - -
2	The conditions of my life are great.		Which conditions are valuable to you? - - -
3	I am satisfied for the most part.		What is missing? - - -
4	My life is going along well.		Except for...? - - -
5	I think I've gotten what I want in life.		What is missing? - - -
6	My life is close to my ideal.		What would make it ideal? - - -
7	I have the important things in life.		Name three things that could impact your answer: - - -
8	If I had it to do over again, I wouldn't change hardly anything.		What would you change? - - -
9	My life is just right.		What makes it "right"? - - -
10	I have a good life.		How do you define "good"? - - -

Adapted from Emmons & Griffin, S. 1985, The Satisfaction with Life Scale.

Additional reflections for higher-order needs/wants are available in the next chapter on Values.

Week 3 ~ How Am I Doing?

It's common to call up a friend and say, "*how are you doing*?". However, asking ourselves the same question can feel superficial. After all, we're in our head and body so we *know* where we're "*at*", right? Not necessarily. Emotions and feelings can be deceiving, and stress and distress can block our ability to access whatever logic may exist in our brain. As we busy ourselves with checking everyone else's boxes and trying to measure up, whatever we conceive our "*status*" to be, it's a healthy practice to be intentional with ourselves as well.

Over the course of the next few days, look at your activities, experiences, thoughts, and feelings through the lens of the "*needs*" you've identified in yourself. Write down one example of each that related to your need and any other observations you made. There are prompts listed after Day 7 that may be helpful to think about as well.

Day 1

_____

_____

_____

_____

_____

Day 2

_____

_____

_____

_____

Day 3

_____

_____

_____

_____

Day 4

_____

_____

_____

_____
_____

Day 5

_____
_____
_____
_____
_____

Day 6

_____
_____
_____
_____
_____

Day 7

_____
_____
_____
_____
_____

What are some of the things that make a day feel "*normal*" to you – what do you do, others do, types of events, food, work, school, dog walking, TV shows, habits, weather, or other activities?

_____
_____
_____
_____
_____
_____

What's your day like when some of those don't occur?

_____
_____
_____
_____
_____

Are some of them more important than others?

_____
_____
_____
_____
_____
_____
_____

Are there ones that have a specific timing of the day that matters, like first thing in the morning or before you go to bed, that you "must" do in order to feel "OK"?

_____
_____
_____
_____
_____
_____
_____

Are there ones that you'd like to change or new ones to incorporate, if so, what are they?

_____
_____
_____
_____
_____
_____
_____

When would be the most important time of day, or in the week, for you to do a check-in with yourself to recalibrate or recharge? _____

Other observations?

_____
_____
_____
_____
_____
_____

"Mindfulness checks in on the location of your mind, brain, and body to make sure they're all in the same time-space."

– Dr. Vic

Week 4 ~ Prioritizing Needs

Based on what you have identified in previous weeks, try to summarize your findings and set a plan to make sure you are prioritizing your needs. You can paperclip this section to serve as a reminder and easy reference later on. Here are some prompts to help you get started.

Your basic internal and physiological needs are (see your Basic Needs Inventory):

_____
_____
_____
_____
_____

In order to meet your needs, you must remember to:

_____
_____
_____
_____
_____

Your higher-order needs are (see Life Satisfaction Inventory):

_____
_____
_____
_____
_____

Prioritizing your needs requires that you fit yourself into your day and can include:

- ✓ Rejecting cognitive/behaviorally conditioned feelings of guilt or self-inflicted reprimands.
- ✓ Recognizing and challenging the "*should's*" they pop up: *should according to whom*?
- ✓ Validating yourself by not comparing to who may be more "*deserving*". You matter.
- ✓ Minding your life / work balance – don't take work home, physically or in your mind.
- ✓ Asking for help meeting your needs from a partner, colleagues, friends, or family.
- ✓ Setting your priorities first thing in the morning. *If you get one thing done today what will be most important to keeping yourself on course*?

Are there other strategies that you know can work for you to check in and make sure your needs are met? (As you discover more, return to this space to keep adding to the list).

✓ _____

✓ _____

✓ _____

✓ _____

✓ _____

✓ _____

✓ _____

✓ _____

✓ _____

✓ _____

What will be your new "should rules" for prioritizing your needs daily and weekly? (Make sure you include higher-order wants for life satisfaction. For example, setting aside a day a week or each month to do something fun and meaningful that inspires and recharges you).

_____

_____

_____

_____

_____

_____

_____

_____

_____

_____

_____

_____

_____

_____

_____

_____

_____

April ~ Values

"Put The Big Rocks In First." ~ Dr. Vic

If there were no limitations on what you could do today, what would you choose? You may be familiar with the *"rocks in the jar"* story. I don't know the official title but the gist of it was that a professor brought a big glass jar to class and three plastic zip bags. One with big stones, one with little stones, and one with sand. He said all of the contents could fit into the one jar but that there was a trick to it. He asked the class to discuss which bag needed to go in first to make it work. After some discussion and range of suggestions, he conducted a demonstration to show that the only way to fit them all in was by adding the big rocks first to then allow the smaller stuff to sift in between.

Now, I don't know if this is a true story nor if it actually works that way, but it provides a good visual for everyday life. Only by putting in the *"big rocks"* first can we feel a sense of fulfillment if the less important stuff doesn't make it into our day. Think about it. If you reflect on today or yesterday, what was most important to you? Getting to work? Spending time with a partner? Walking the dog? Securing tickets to the show on Saturday? Were you successful in doing it all? Probably not.

So, which parts could have been left out and the day would have been fine without them? How much distress or disappointment did you feel about things you didn't get to? What did you have control over and what was out of your control? Which ones represent the big rocks, little ones, and the sand? For this month, you'll have opportunity to focus on what matters to you and finding the best approach for making important things fit, maybe even discovering what has little value in the bigger scheme of things.

What you value drives almost everything you do, even when you don't realize it. However, what most of us do is put the sand in first. The little distractions, phone attention, social media scrolling, the internal chatter of the mind between wants, needs, what should be, what's possible, and what's screaming in your face. Every day is your jar and the tasks this month are designed to:

1. Help you define your values by categories.
2. Identify your big rocks and set layers of prioritization.
3. Navigate distractions to stay focused on what matters.
4. Set a plan for intentional use of your values in everyday life.

The most important things in life to me are:

_____
_____
_____
_____
_____
_____
_____
_____
_____
_____
_____
_____
_____
_____
_____
_____
_____
_____
_____
_____
_____
_____
_____
_____
_____
_____
_____
_____
_____
_____
_____
_____
_____

Week 1 ~ Categorical Values

This week you'll be considering some common categorical values. As with other journaling exercises take some time during the week to reflect on different days to identify things that were *meaningful* versus *meaningless*. You can use the table below for reference. Rate the categories by 1-10 where "1" is the most important and "10" the least or it doesn't pertain to you at all. Don't worry about having too many "1's" or "10's", try to be as honest as you can in this stage of the process. Consider why the area is important to you, is it because of what's important to someone else or does it hold special meaning for you, something you enjoy? Lastly, write down an example of an activity that relates to the category.

Rate	Category/Value	Your Examples	Why?
	Achievement, success		
	Activism, advocacy		
	Adventure		
	Alone time		
	Community involvement		
	Creating art and self-expression		
	Cultural belonging, diversity		
	A clean and organized home		
	Education, learning, knowledge		
	Exploring, researching		
	Fairness, justice, equality		
	Financial security, wealth		
	Flexibility, spontaneity		
	Fun, humor		
	Going out for entertainment		
	Health and wellness		
	Helping others		
	How I look, hygiene, appearance		
	Journaling, writing		
	Leisure, free time, relaxation		
	Nature, climate, conservation		
	Online entertaining, gaming		
	Peace, harmony, balance		
	Physical activity, exercise, walking		
	Politics, news		
	Reading		
	Recognition, popularity, fame		
	Religion, spirituality, faith		
	Respect, honor, loyalty, integrity		
	Routine, stability, order, organization		
	Self-improvement, growth		
	Social media and online connectedness		
	Social status and role		
	Sports or other hobby's		
	Staying at home		

Rate	Category/Value	Your Examples	Why?
	Teamwork		
	Time with family or relatives		
	Time with friends		
	Time with pets		
	Traveling		
	Volunteering		
	Work, career, employment, job		
	Other:		
	Other:		
	Other:		

Which ones did you rate #1, #2, or #3 but don't often fit into a week or day?

_____

_____

_____

_____

_____

_____

_____

For those that you noted that the "*why*" is based on what someone else has asked of you, or it's a family/friend value, make a note of that here.

_____

_____

_____

_____

_____

What were your #1's?

☐ _____

☐ _____

☐ _____

☐ _____

☐ _____

☐ _____

☐ _____

What were your "#2's"?

☐ _____
☐ _____
☐ _____
☐ _____
☐ _____
☐ _____
☐ _____

What were your "#3's"?

☐ _____
☐ _____
☐ _____
☐ _____
☐ _____
☐ _____
☐ _____

Other observations?

_____
_____
_____
_____
_____
_____
_____
_____
_____
_____
_____
_____
_____
_____
_____
_____
_____
_____

"If you don't like where you are, move, you're not a tree."
- Unknown

Week 2 ~ Primary v. Secondary

Values can be primary or secondary and they can host conflict within themselves, with time, with you, or within relationships in which case you may feel off, out of balance, or experience some form of cognitive dissonance. For example, maybe you're making a decision that your parents, or a partner don't agree with. You value their opinion but *really* want to do your own thing. Maybe you're worried about the consequences; you value peace over conflict or have a need to be perceived as a *"good person"* so you worry about rejection. Maybe you fear being labeled as *"argumentative"*, so which of those things that are also important to you will sway your decision most? Your inner compass or external controls? What is most in alignment with what you identified last week as #1, #2, or even #3? This is the difference between primary and secondary.

Making this distinction can be helpful when decisions are on the table. Whether it's choosing between taking your kids to an event versus demands of work or having a wet burrito instead of a healthy chicken salad, minding your values can be tricky. For example, one of your #1's may be *"freedom"* and the other *"health"*. Clearly there can be a conflict of even having to choose between a burrito and salad. One meets the *"health"* value and the other meets the *"freedom"* value. Which one do you want to honor more in that moment? What will motivate you to choose what is *"right"* for you when both meet the criteria for *"right"*? Too often our feelings and lack of self-control can make us do things we later realize were not so right.

In the above scenario, it may be an *"achievement"* value that ends up being the deciding factor. As in, meeting goals or needs that you have set for yourself, accountability with a friend, or a health membership. Deciding in advance what will rule for you by understanding your layered and contextual motivational values can help you do what you will truly value as *"right"*. The more times you do the right thing the easier it will be to keep doing it.

Consider a day in recent times where you had a good or great day, what values did you incorporate that day? Were they intentionally planned or the result of an opportunity that opened up? Were any of them #1 or #2 on your list?

_____

_____

_____

_____

_____

_____

_____

_____

Consider a day in recent times when you had to make a difficult decision or choose between two conflicting values, what were they and how did you make your choice? Are there other times when what was primary this time is secondary?

_____
_____
_____
_____
_____
_____
_____
_____
_____
_____
_____

What role did *goals*, *needs*, or *logic* have in making your decision?

_____
_____
_____
_____
_____
_____
_____

What role did *stress*, *emotions*, or *self-control* have in making your decision?

_____
_____
_____
_____
_____
_____
_____

Any other observations?

_____
_____
_____
_____
_____

Charting Needs, Values, and Goals (NVGs)

In this exercise, enter your highest Needs/Wants according to what you identified in the previous chapter. Do the same for Values from this chapter and enter the ones that meet a #1 rating. Include some of your most important Goals in the last column from the very first chapter. Then consider what you actually DO on a regular basis to align the three. For example, if you spend a lot of time online yet are trying to manage your time or you feel bad about not supporting a friend when they call every day to complain about their job yet you want to manage your boundaries. If you have few friends or lack availability of other hobbies besides being online, these can be tough decision points as to what to prioritize. Then take a moment to see which align and which ones may be in conflict. You can use the checkmark column if you want to track changes you make to align your NVG's. Here's an example:

Needs	Values *(Thoughts/Beliefs)*	Goals
Freedom to do what I want	A "good" person has self-control	Manage time better
Belonging	A "good" friend texts back and supports their friend all the time	Manage boundaries

Congruence Chart

Needs		Values		Goals

What would you need to change in order to align your NVGs?

_____

_____

_____

_____

_____
_____
_____
_____
_____
_____
_____
_____

Now, do a little test with yourself tomorrow to see how you can configure the day in a way that allows you to tackle distractions and fit in one of your top value items. Return here and reflect on what worked, what didn't work, and any changes you'll need to make before trying again.

_____
_____
_____
_____
_____
_____
_____

"How to cope with a set-back?
Don't let it stop you from moving forward." - Unknown

Week 3 ~ Who's The Boss?

Where did your values come from and who sets the rules when it comes to making your values a reality in your life? It's easy to blame all the distractions or life's demands, but as difficult as some choices may be, we always have them. Even on bad days when we get hung up on one thing that went wrong. We play the scenario endlessly in our mind, feel bad, talk about it with everyone, and accept defeat by doing nothing else that day to even try to refocus. At other times we follow old implicit rules set by others. After all, grandma had five kids, took care of grandpa, plowed the field, did the laundry, and cooked dinner, right?! Sometimes we're unreasonable and unrealistic, old rules can be irrelevant and sometimes we're out of timing.

So, who's the boss? Who wears the pants in your life? I can guarantee you that at the end of it you'll want to look back and see the most important things consuming it, not regrets. But accomplishing that will require everyday vigilance and ongoing adjustment of time, resources, goals, and needs. There is never going to be that one thing that makes it all work out perfectly, but you can set rules for yourself, simple and easy to remember *value-rules*.

Think of these rules like those that guide the superhero movie scene where the superhero is faced with a life-or-death situation. Who should the superhero choose to save, the people in the tram dangling off the side of the cliff, or disarm the bomb that will decimate an entire city? Sometimes it comes down to a moral high ground of what is considered just and fair at other times it's about weighing variables of time, resources, effort, and the lesser of two consequences (or evils). Similarly, you must decide what that looks like by understanding where your values originate and what to stand by and what to discard: morals, ethics, or consequences etc.

In previous weeks you identified the #1 things that are important to you. Take a moment to write down what you consider to be the top five:

1. _____
2. _____
3. _____
4. _____
5. _____

Family Values & Rules

Think about your childhood family (mom, dad, or siblings etc.) who had those same five values?

#1 _____
#2 _____
#3 _____
#4 _____
#5 _____

How were those values communicated to you? Where did they come from? To discover the answer, you can explore the following sentences:

My mom or dad always (or never) said/did _____
_____
_____
_____
_____
_____

My grandpa/grandma always (or never) said/did _____
_____
_____
_____
_____
_____

I had an uncle/aunt who always (or never) said/did _____
and it influenced me and my family by _____
_____
_____
_____
_____
_____

When I was little we always (or never) _____
_____
_____
_____
_____
_____

Think of some childhood memories before age 16. What were the main rules and things that were important to you or your family then? Holidays, events, daily chores, people? What is still important to you today?

_____
_____
_____
_____
_____

Regrets

Regrets are basically things you wish could have been different. While it's easy to stay there and feel the pain of loss, it may be a better approach to finish grieving and begin to figure out which things you have control over and set a plan of action for the future to ensure you do all you can to get those big rocks in first.

What has prevented you from following your values in the past? Which ones?

_____

_____

_____

_____

_____

I always thought that if I didn't/did then _____

_____

_____

_____

_____

_____

Do you have any regrets? Describe them and how they relate to what's important to you.

_____

_____

_____

_____

_____

What are you doing that you feel good about now and what do you need to keep doing to make room for your values every day?

_____

_____

_____

_____

_____

What would your future self, need or appreciate if you did now?

_____

_____

_____

_____

Daily View

In the previous week 2 you selected one day to observe and test the values you had selected. Over the next few days, consider your *thoughts*, *feelings*, *people* you encounter, *experiences*, *events*, your *actions*, and any *regrets*, then make a note of what seemed valuable each day relatively. Did you prioritize the way you'd like? What could you have changed to make the day better?

Day 1

_____

_____

_____

_____

_____

_____

_____

_____

_____

_____

_____

_____

_____

Day 2

_____

_____

_____

_____

_____

_____

_____

_____

_____

_____

_____

_____

Day 3

_____

Day 4

Day 5

_____

_____

Day 6

_____

_____

_____

_____

_____

_____

_____

_____

_____

_____

_____

_____

_____

Day 7

_____

_____

_____

_____

_____

_____

_____

_____

_____

_____

_____

Week 4 ~ Applying Values

Minding your values and fitting the big rocks in can be a big challenge but It's necessary if you want to be authentic and feel a sense of congruence in life, with others, and within yourself. Any comparing and pleasing you try to do won't matter if you aren't enjoying and honoring yourself in some way. Every day you can make sure to find something that keeps you going or moves you in the right direction towards your dreams and goals. No one can do it for you and the happiness of doing something meaningful to you, is up to you.

For this weeks' tasks take some time to summarize your findings from the past three weeks and set a plan that you can use as a reminder of what matters to you. There is a popular question that can be useful in navigating the busyness of the day that someone translated into an acronym, *"W.I.N."*. It stands for *"What's Important Now?"*. Getting in the habit of catching yourself doing or being consumed with thoughts about things that don't hold value to you and asking that question can help you get back on track.

Primary Values

#1 items that have authority over anything else and must be prioritized in decision-making:

☐ _____
☐ _____
☐ _____

#1 items that must fit into the week are:

☐ _____
☐ _____
☐ _____

My morning focus: "if I only get one thing done today it must be": _____
_____
_____

Secondary Values

Your top #2 and #3 items are:

☐ _____
☐ _____
☐ _____

Value Indicators

A major indicator that you are not honoring your values can be if you begin to feel resentment towards someone or something. If you've had this occur in the past, you may want to make a note of it here and identify what values you ignored and substituted with someone else's. What can you do differently to avoid that in the future?

_____
_____
_____
_____
_____
_____
_____
_____
_____
_____

Any other observations that you want to keep in mind?

_____
_____
_____
_____
_____
_____
_____
_____
_____
_____
_____
_____
_____
_____
_____
_____
_____
_____
_____

May ~ Beliefs & Motivation

"Whether you believe you can or believe you can't, you are correct." ~ Unknown

How do we come to believe what we believe? What is it that makes us think we can do something? What propels us to move forward when things aren't going as expected? There are basically two ways we make sense of things; by matching external input with internal information. What you are experiencing against a backdrop of what has been. However, both of those are subjective not objective. There is much more to know. So how can we understand what to believe and obtain motivation? The first step is to not settle and park on anything unless it fits with your goals, needs, and values.

I'm sure you have seen, and maybe explored, some of the many online self-assessments to *determine* what your mindset or personality type is, what your relationship or attachment style is, communication style, or even your IQ. While they may claim to be objective tests they are based on norms, comparisons with others. Unfortunately, they can leave you with nothing more than a label and a score. For example, what if a test tells you that you're an introvert with an IQ of 105 who has an anxious attachment style with passive-aggressive communication tendencies, and you live within a prevention mindset. Or worse, that you qualify for a mental disorder, a disease. What are you going to do with that? What are you going to believe about yourself or your future? What will you believe you can or can't do because of those results? How does it impact your attitude in various situations?

This is a dangerous matching game. It leaves the door open for *congruence* and *self-fulfilling prophecy* to have the final say and that can be a mental stop sign that keeps you stuck or spinning. While a label and score can seem like you finally have all the answers, it can also disempower you. As much as we strive for certainty, the one thing we can rely on is the capacity for the human mind to change, if we allow it to. Whether that takes place by trauma impact, medicine, physiological changes, surgery, or by cognitive restructuring through exposure to new knowledge and altered effort, virtually anything can be possible but only if you believe it is. Beliefs are as Einstein, an original influencer, said:

"Everybody is a genius. But if you judge a fish by its ability to climb a tree, it will live its whole life believing that it is stupid."

The lesson here is to be careful what you expose your mind to and believe. Your motivational system is comprised of your thoughts, beliefs, and feelings about experiences that you've had and your relative processing about cause and effect. Within that there can be biases, attribution errors, and appraisal misalignments. This is not to say that there is anything wrong, it just means that the set of information you have received while living in the world has taught you to make meaning of what you can and can't do in a certain way. That information impacts your everyday decisions of whether to retreat, remain still, or take action, all of which is malleable.

This month you'll have opportunity to reflect on what makes you tick, how you make sense of things, and discover what motivates you in order to leverage what is working for you and/or change what is not. No matter what label you've been living under, if you aren't finding yourself high on life satisfaction then it may be time to explore a new label and set a new direction. Only you can do that by what you believe is possible for you.

The steps to breaking down and understanding the impact of your beliefs and motivational factors involve four tasks:

1. Taking inventory of what your mind has been believing and consider it in the context of others and your foundations.

2. Identify and define your motives and motivation.

3. Evaluate your beliefs and their effectiveness.

4. Set a plan to gain more effective and intentional control over your beliefs.

Week 1 ~ Beliefs Inventory

What do your beliefs do to, and for you anyway? Beliefs are layered systems with many variable contexts. To simplify, *"beliefs"* help you maintain safety; cognitively, psychologically, emotionally, and physically. For example, if you've had several bad experiences with chairs breaking, you are far less likely to believe they are safe than other people who've not had any problems. This may impact your behavior when someone says, *"sit down"*. Instead of sitting down you may examine the chair and question it's construction. Similarly, beliefs can keep you from doing what you really want and meeting your own needs by acting like blinders.

In the Beliefs Table below there are statements that represent common beliefs people have. Read through each of them and give some thought to what that looks like in your own life, whether they are relevant to you or someone you know, and if it's something you believed in the past that has now changed. For example, which ones do you feel strongly about that maybe conflict with a close relative or friend? Which ones are you on the fence about and why? What would be the tipping point? Which ones keep you from doing things in life? And if you changed your belief in the past, what's to stop you from doing so now?

Belief	If this is a current belief, provide an example and its impact.	I used to believe this	I know others who believe this
I believe I am safe			
You can't trust anyone			
I don't feel like I deserve …			
I can't be myself around people			
I can't trust my own judgement / instincts			
People are wonderful			
People come through for me			
I can't control myself			

Belief	If this is a current belief, provide an example and its impact.	I used to believe this	I know others who believe this
I could do serious damage to someone			
No one listens to me			
People can't really change			
Everyone struggles			
Trusting people is not smart			
I'm not worth much because _____			
You can't believe what people say			
The world is a dangerous place			
People are no good			
Everybody has a purpose in life			
Things happen for a reason			
People never show who they really are			
Life is what it is and then you die			
Strong people don't need to ask for help			
I'm a good person			
People don't keep promises			
People are always trying to control others			

Belief	If this is a current belief, provide an example and its impact.	I used to believe this	I know others who believe this
You must love yourself to love others			
People can be good at heart			
Its ok to be alone			
Needing help is a sign of weakness			
Bad things happen to bad people			
Good things happen to good people			
People are there when I need them			
No one *really* knows me			
I can usually figure things out			
If people knew me, they wouldn't like me			

Adapted from Laurie Pearlman, 2003, Belief Scale, Western Psychological Services.

Societal and Core Beliefs

Although the world is becoming increasingly global, we all come from a platform of family systems that have evolved through socio-cultural practices and beliefs. These can be traditions, spiritual beliefs, beliefs about morals and ethics, how to behave in certain situations, and even what to think about life and experiences. Consider the following prompts to dig into your socio-cultural vault of original belonging and reflect on how that fits into your current lifestyle and orientation. Your responses can be an elaboration on what you discovered in the Beliefs Table or entirely different observations.

Family and cultural morals and ethics in my childhood included:

_____

_____

_____
_____
_____
_____
_____
_____
_____
_____

Sayings and phrases often repeated in my family and upbringing were:

_____
_____
_____
_____
_____
_____
_____
_____
_____

I believe it's right to:

_____
_____
_____
_____
_____

I believe it's wrong to:

_____
_____
_____
_____

I believe people are generally:

_____
_____
_____
_____

I define a "good" person as:

_____
_____
_____
_____
_____

Because of my beliefs I don't:

_____
_____
_____
_____
_____
_____
_____
_____
_____
_____

Because of my beliefs I do:

_____
_____
_____
_____
_____

Any other observations or important beliefs such as religious or professional ethical ones that serve as a guide for you?

_____
_____
_____
_____
_____
_____
_____
_____
_____
_____

"What do you think it means? Could it mean something else or is your mind made up? Be careful what you settle on and what you allow into long-term memory for later use and interpretation. You can't delete a memory." – Dr. Vic

Week 2 ~ Motives and Motivation

Separating motive from motivation can seem a little like splitting hairs but there are important differences; while motives are achievement-oriented motivations are belief-oriented. Your motive for being nice to someone may be to get them to like you but the reason you get out of bed in the morning is not to get that person to like you. However, if you are well-liked and have a good support group that may be motivation enough to get out of bed.

In that way, a motivation can encourage you to keep going when things feel impossible while a motive alone cannot do so if you don't believe that continuing to strive will make a difference. Identifying how these two play out in your life is the goal for this week.

Over the next few days, consider your *thoughts*, *feelings*, *people* you encounter, *experiences*, *events*, yours and other's *actions*, and *reasons* you did what you did. Whether it's what you chose for breakfast, to say to someone, whether to lend a hand, what to think, to do after work etc. Then make a note of your observations each day. What motivated you to either help others or yourself to press on? What was your motive and motivation? And what did you expect or hope it would accomplish?

Day 1

_____
_____
_____
_____
_____
_____
_____
_____
_____
_____

Day 2

_____
_____
_____
_____
_____
_____
_____
_____
_____

Day 3

_____
_____
_____
_____
_____
_____
_____
_____
_____
_____

Day 4

_____
_____
_____
_____
_____
_____
_____
_____
_____
_____

Day 5

_____
_____
_____
_____
_____
_____
_____
_____
_____
_____

Day 6

_____
_____

Day 7

Any other observations?

*"Never stop believing because
miracles happen every day." - Unknown*

Week 3 ~ What would you do if only ....

Beliefs and motivation can keep you stuck depending on how you made sense of negative feedback experiences. The tasks for this week will center around identifying external events and experiences that may have contributed to a false sense of self and potential for you. These are motivation-killers. Follow the prompts through the course of the week to let them simmer over time and different situations then write down things that resonate with you, even if they seem impossible, be honest in your reflections of their impact on your day, your actions, and how you move through life. The overarching question is what would you do if only _____ ?

Comparisons & Perfection

What are your comparison points? Some of the culprits that keep us from moving forward are our own ideals, thoughts, and perceptions of how things *"should look or be"* relative to success. Here are some things to consider in order to get to the bottom of motives and beliefs.

What do others do that you could never do but want to do:

_____
_____
_____
_____
_____

What do you think others do better than you, why?

_____
_____
_____
_____
_____

How do you define perfection?

_____
_____
_____
_____
_____

What are the ideal circumstances under which you feel good about yourself and life?

_____
_____
_____

_____
_____
_____

External Feedback

Competence can be one of the more significant areas that keep you from believing you CAN do something. Some of that ties into comparisons, at other times its how we perceive others as successful because we see their end-results as more confident and able. The reality is always that they had to battle it out with their own self-esteem, goals, and values to believe they could before doing what they do. We _can_ do the same but not if we get stuck on negative feedback and only looking at the results. Unfortunately, that is what we are trained to do since birth. We look to our caregivers to see whether we should cry when we fall down, be scared of the thunder, and even when to get angry and upset for big or small things rather than stay calm. Our entire system is designed by our early life experiences, and no one teaches us when we should stop looking, or how to, distinguish between us and them – how to set up our internal compass to navigate our own path. As a result, many of us continue to look for external feedback as indicators of our capacity, potential, and whether we're OK or not. However, it is a false sense of security and digging up that root can take some effort and it starts by awareness.

In this exercise take some time to finish the following sentences to gauge how reliant and in which situations you tend to look to others for input on how you are doing.

I've always been told that _____
_____
_____
_____
_____
_____
_____
_____

I've always thought that I couldn't because _____
_____
_____
_____
_____
_____
_____
_____

What has others said about you and what was that like for you? How did it change your self-perception? Was/is it true?

_____
_____
_____
_____
_____
_____
_____

What has made you feel motivated the past week, month, year that made a difference?

_____
_____
_____
_____
_____

What has someone said to you or about you that made you feel motivated and encouraged?

_____
_____
_____
_____
_____

Internal Compass

What is your internal compass set to? What is your "true" north that guides you? Consider what your answers were in the grid the first week and what you observed over the seven days in week 3. What thoughts, fears, feelings, or other internal sensory information guided you most; which moved you forward, and which held you back from taking action when you wanted to?

_____
_____
_____
_____
_____
_____
_____
_____
_____

What do you believe about yourself now that may have changed over time? What did that evolution of change look like? What had to happen to change your mind?

_____

_____

_____

_____

_____

Is there something that stands out to you in your experiences where you tried something, and it didn't work out as you had planned? How did that impact your choices with other opportunities?

_____

_____

_____

_____

_____

Is there something in your history that you tried, and it did work out? What was that impact?

_____

_____

_____

_____

_____

What makes you go to work, call a friend, ask for help?

_____

_____

_____

_____

_____

What stops you from taking action: saying, doing, or thinking and believing something?

_____

_____

_____

_____

_____

As a result of my reflections, I want to change:

_____

_____

_____

_____

Potential

Potential cannot be fully realized until all effort has been exerted and exhausted physically, which in essence has an indefinite trajectory, at least until there is something that stops it. Like a rollercoaster that reaches the top, there is no other place to go but downhill. Its mission is complete, and the results achieved. These are the laws of kinetic energy, and they also apply to you. Realizing your potential is not possible until you keep moving forward and something stops you physically. Even then you can find a detour and reroute. Too often what stops us is not outside of us, but inside – what we believe and our motives. So, what has been stopping you?

For this exercise you'll be doing a bit of research. Choose someone that you admire or look up to who has accomplished something that you'd also want to accomplish, then consider the following prompts:

What are they doing now that you aren't (their beliefs, efforts, routines etc.)?

_____
_____
_____
_____
_____

What did they do or go through to get there (their effort and timeline from start to now?

_____
_____
_____
_____
_____

Was there a process they followed, if so, what motivated them?

_____
_____
_____
_____
_____

What is missing for you, in order to take some steps and do something, to establish a process, or get motivated in similar ways? What is stopping you (thoughts, beliefs, or routines)?

_____
_____
_____
_____
_____

*"Believing the best feels better than believing the worst.
How are you feeling?" – Dr. Vic*

Week 4 ~ Gaining Control: The Plan

In your reflections the past few weeks, what stands out to you the most and what ?

_____
_____
_____
_____
_____
_____
_____
_____
_____
_____
_____
_____

What do you believe you have control over in the various areas you have reflected on the past few weeks?

_____
_____
_____
_____
_____
_____
_____
_____

Patterns

Did you identify any specific patterns of motives or beliefs that fuel expectations you may have?

_____
_____
_____
_____
_____
_____
_____
_____
_____

Did you identify any specific patterns of motivation; what gets you up in the morning or keeps you pressing on during difficult times?

_____

_____

_____

_____

_____

_____

_____

_____

Redesigning Beliefs and Motivations

In the first week you examined some common beliefs that can impact what you do and your movement in life. In this last segment you'll be deciding what to do with those beliefs. Here is a revised version of that table. After all your reflections, what would you want to change, if anything? Capture some of your notes in the righthand column then follow the prompts for some last reflections to set up a plan for reaching your new potential.

Belief	Keep, Discard, or Reframe?
I believe I am safe	
You can't trust anyone	
I don't feel like I deserve …	
I can't be myself around people	
I can't trust my own judgement / instincts	
People are wonderful	
People come through for me	
I can't control myself	
I could do serious damage to someone	

Belief	Keep, Discard, or Reframe?
No one listens to me	
People can't really change	
Everyone struggles	
Trusting people is not smart	
I'm not worth much because _____	
You can't believe what people say	
The world is a dangerous place	
People are no good	
Everybody has a purpose in life	
Things happen for a reason	
People never show who they really are	
Life is what it is and then you die	
Strong people don't need to ask for help	
I'm a good person	
People don't keep promises	
People are always trying to control others	
You must love yourself to love others	

Belief	Keep, Discard, or Reframe?
People can be good at heart	
Its ok to be alone	
Needing help is a sign of weakness	
Bad things happen to bad people	
Good things happen to good people	
People are there when I need them	
No one *really* knows me	
I can usually figure things out	
If people knew me, they wouldn't like me	

Adapted from Laurie Pearlman, 2003, Belief Scale, Western Psychological Services.

Which ones did you decide are outdated?

_____

_____

_____

_____

_____

Which ones did you decide need some adjusting and reframing?

_____

_____

_____

_____

_____

Which ones did you decide were *"keepers"*?

_____

_____

_____

_____

_____

_____

_____

_____

_____

Keepers

To make the changes you want to make and have more effective control of your motivation there are several strategies you can use. Here are some examples:

☐ Set small achievable goals daily. If you can manage something in the moment you can build on that to manage bigger things. It's about developing a habit in thought and action that in and of itself motivates you. That internal compass.

☐ Take charge of your day first thing in the morning. People who tend to meet their goals and stay motivated guard their time and resources carefully by relying on strategy more than reaction. How can you set a plan for the day that sets you up for success and keeps you focused? Believing the best? Having a power phrase? Remembering something good someone said about you? A success from the past? A process that worked before?

☐ Notice when you feel discouraged; is it because of what you are believing and expecting? Can you change it to build up hope instead? Look at your "keepers" and remind yourself of something positive. In the next chapter you'll be identifying more of those strengths which you can use to fuel your plan. Here are some blank spaces to add your own thoughts and tools for believing, motivating yourself, and challenging your motives and capture what works for you for later reference:

☐ _____

_____

☐ _____

_____

☐ _____

_____

☐ _____

_____

Beliefs that fuel positive psychological health and wellbeing include:

☐ Believing the best about situations and people.

☐ That you will figure it out and find a solution.

☐ You are ok and you will get through it.

☐ Knowledge empowers. Everything you experience is more information, use it wisely.

☐ Patience is a virtue and sometimes time is the only answer.

☐ You're good enough and you matter.

☐ You're doing the best you can with what you know.

☐ It doesn't have to be perfect.

☐ Life has its ups and downs. Some days good, some days not so good.

☐ It's ok to be yourself.

☐ All things have a way of working themselves out. Do what you can.

☐ No matter the mistake or wrong step, you can learn from it to become the best version of you.

☐ You don't have to have it all figured out to move forward.

☐ You have something important to offer the world. Look for it.

☐ Your efforts will be worth it. Stick with it.

☐ You deserve to feel good and be happy. The responsibility to make it happen is yours.

☐ Are there other phrases or beliefs that help you feel empowered?

☐ _____

☐ _____

☐ _____

☐ _____

☐ _____

☐ _____

☐ _____

☐ _____

☐ _____

☐ _____

June ~ Strengths

*"What you look for you will find and
what you magnify will become bigger." ~ Dr. Vic*

In the last chapter you probably saw a glimpse of your strengths by examining your beliefs and motivations, those things that drive what you do and how you feel. Looking for our strength is definitely not our strong-suit but it's the most effective way to override the demands that life can put on us, or that we put on ourselves. Beyond mere positivity and good vibes, strength is about having the power to lift yourself out of internal and external situations that are compromising your wellbeing. It's also about fueling yourself for everyday living.

The process for seeking out strength begins in the mind. Yes, I think we're all somewhat tired of hearing that we must *change our thinking to change our life*. However, there is no other way around it. In order to do anything, you must first conceive of it in your thoughts. Additionally, research states that it's important to know "*how*" something is possible in order to believe and take action on it. Whether you think you are strong or not, you have made it this far in life and part of the reason for that involves your strength, will power, and determination as well as external resources.

In this chapter you'll be exploring what you can leverage during difficulties, how to maintain your gains when you find them, and how to advance to a new level of confidence. While we tend to have no problem talking about and pointing to a problem, the only way to feel strong and empowered is to focus on what works to move you forward.

Yes, it is important to define the problem but no matter how you try to fix old wounds, even yesterday's, today is a new day and you have a choice of where to send your mind; where you have control or where you don't. Whatever strength you had yesterday is no longer available and in order to feel your best your mind and body must be in the same place. Finding strength for each day requires a catalog of resources, a mental scorecard that doesn't look at what "*was*" but what "*can be*" so to do what you "*can*" right now. The four tasks this month explore:

1. What you do well.
2. Your environmental strengths and resources.
3. Coping mechanisms.
4. Power tools.

"There is a logic that philosophy, concepts, and labels can't understand or explain and that's the practical steps to living everyday life. That's up to you to decide." – Dr. Vic

Week 1 ~ What You Do Well

If someone asked you what you like to do, what would you say? Would you attach a qualifier to it? Like, *"I love to play soccer but I'm not very good at it"* or *"I love to write but I'm no writer or published author"*. When we think of *what we do well* we tend to go down the same rabbit hole. *"I dabble a little"* or *"I tried it a few times but ..."*. However, what you do well has less to do with what others think of it and more about how something is working for you.

For example, if playing soccer makes you happy then it's working for you every time you do it or think about it, even if no one else understands or appreciates it. Now, let's say that being appreciated and recognized for achievement is one of your higher-order needs, then there would need to be a match between the two for happiness or satisfaction to occur. In order to understand what you do well and apply it, you must combine the two – what you like to do and recognizing the benefits YOU derive from it. There are a wealth of options and tools online for understanding your strengths today. If you are seeing a counselor, they may also be able to provide you with helpful strength assessment and strength development tools. This can be life changing. If you are like most of us who have spent an inordinate amount of time with Dr. Google to find a diagnostic fit for *"symptoms"* then changing those search habits to find strength inventories and strength building techniques will definitely be a psychologically useful change of scenery.

To kick off this month's journaling, you'll begin with a blank slate. There are seven sections for making your notes, one for each day of the week. As with other exercises in this book, you'll be spending some time monitoring and observing yourself to take inventory. For each day try to have a lens of *"empowered"* that takes into account events, your thoughts, feelings, and actions that fuel you. Here are some prompts to help you think it through as you reflect on your day:

1. Was there a time during the day when you felt best or better than other times? What were you doing, what was happening around you, and how long did it last?
2. Was there something that you did better than someone else and how did that impact how you felt?
3. If you felt successful during the day, what did you attribute that success to?
4. What did you feel proud of or what can you trust about yourself?
5. If you spent time online, what types of positive experiences did you have, or information did you see?
6. What did you do that no one noticed but you thought went really well?
7. Were you able to help someone else, what did you do and how did they respond?
8. What did you do in your spare time? How did that feel?
9. Was there a time during the day when you felt energized or inspired?
10. Was there anything you set out to do that you completed? What was that like?
11. Was there something you did that contributed to something going well?
12. What was easy to do?
13. If you faced a conflict or challenge, how did you get through it?
14. Was there anything that made you think/feel like you made a difference?
15. What did you value about yourself?

Day 1

_____
_____
_____
_____
_____
_____
_____
_____
_____
_____

Day 2

_____
_____
_____
_____
_____
_____
_____
_____
_____
_____

Day 3

_____
_____
_____
_____
_____
_____
_____
_____
_____

Day 4

_____
_____
_____
_____
_____
_____
_____
_____
_____
_____
_____

Day 5

_____
_____
_____
_____
_____
_____
_____
_____
_____
_____
_____

Day 6

_____
_____
_____
_____
_____
_____
_____
_____
_____
_____
_____

Day 7

_____

_____
_____
_____
_____
_____
_____
_____
_____
_____

Which days for the past week would you count as "*good days*", why?

_____
_____
_____
_____
_____
_____
_____
_____
_____
_____
_____

If you were to design an ideal day, which elements from the past week would be included?

_____
_____
_____
_____
_____
_____
_____
_____
_____
_____
_____
_____
_____
_____
_____

What are some of your accomplishments in life that you did well? Did you graduate high school? Pass a test? Finish a project? Overcome a problem? Get a degree? Get the job? Get an award? Don't be shy – take some time to look back and list the things that you feel proud of and/or were recognized for.

_____
_____
_____
_____
_____
_____
_____
_____
_____
_____
_____
_____

What would your friends, family, or coworkers say you do well?

_____
_____
_____
_____
_____
_____
_____
_____
_____
_____
_____

What would your friends, family, or coworkers recognize as an accomplishment of yours?

_____
_____
_____
_____
_____
_____
_____
_____
_____

Any other observations?

_____
_____
_____
_____
_____
_____
_____
_____
_____
_____
_____
_____
_____
_____
_____
_____
_____
_____
_____
_____
_____
_____
_____
_____
_____
_____
_____
_____
_____
_____
_____
_____
_____
_____
_____
_____

Week 2 ~ Environmental Strengths

A common understanding in cognitive psychology is that nothing can *"make us"* feel anything; that we *choose* our feelings. It is also a common concept in Reality Therapy. While it does hold some truth there is a physiological reality of the brain that can't be ignored. External environmental influences can in fact be key to how we think, feel, and what we do. We see this in Dr. Zimbardo's *Stanford Prison Experiment* in 1971 where *human will* was tested by having to choose between internal morals and deference to external demands and roles. It's also reflected in Lazarus's *Appraisal Theory* and Zajonc's *Mere Exposure Effect*.

However, external influences do not necessarily operate the way we tend to think they do, as in being *"out of our control"* or a *"trigger"* that forces us to *do* or *feel* something. It's actually something we *can* leverage to find control above and beyond what we think we have, although as a *strength* it may be easier said than done.

The undeniable physiological reality of the mind is that it's a network of information that relies on cues to pull up data from its memory bank. Those memories of information, albeit not stored in a single location, consist of feelings, emotions, thoughts, and sensory experiences, and so on. If I say *"umbrella"* it is probably not a word that was on your mind right now yet when you see that word your mind is able to think of associated words and events like rain, puddle, or even sand and sun, as in *"beach umbrella"*. Your mind may even have delivered up a pleasant memory from an experience you had in the rain or on the beach. It's what Freud referred to and used to develop his *"word association"* activity.

This week you'll do a similar type of reflection with things that seem to be associations of influence for you. Using last week's inventory, reflect on each day of journaling and consider these prompts.

Were there times that you felt compromised or overwhelmed? What was going on around you, who was with you, and what were you thinking, feeling, doing?

_____

_____

_____

_____

_____

_____

_____

_____

_____

_____

Which of those things were in your control and out of your control?

_____

_____

_____

_____

_____

_____

_____

Was there something or someone that helped you navigate through it to a better emotional place? What did they do or what happened?

_____

_____

_____

_____

_____

_____

_____

Choose one of your positive experiences from last week, or any other time, how did it start, who was involved, and what impact did it have on your behavior?

_____

_____

_____

_____

_____

_____

_____

Choose a conversation you had with someone that went well, what did they say and what did that make you think of or contribute in a positive way?

_____

_____

_____

_____

_____

_____

_____

In your journaling the past week, if there were there times you felt inspired or energized, what were you doing, others doing, and what was happening? What was it about the experience that made it inspirational?

_____
_____
_____
_____
_____
_____
_____
_____
_____
_____
_____

If you were to list all the resources and external influences that contributed to a good day, experience, or connection last week within your social network or community, what would those be?

_____
_____
_____
_____
_____
_____
_____
_____
_____
_____
_____

Which ones are accessible to you now?

_____
_____
_____
_____
_____
_____
_____
_____
_____
_____

"Don't just do what's easy.
Do what's right, even when it's hard.
The more you practice the easier it gets ...". – Dr. Vic

Week 3 ~ The Process

For everything you do there is a process, whether you realize it and know what it is or not. For example, before you go to the doctor you must make time to call to make the appointment, look at your calendar to match up an availability with the doctor, and perhaps clear it with your insurance company. To cook dinner, you must select a recipe, plan, shop, cook etc.

A process is a sequence of events that leads to a result. While it's easy to identify the steps in the above examples, there is a similar process to thinking and feeling as well – it can be intentional or implicit. For example, there is a process to getting angry and a process to achieving happiness. We tend to think of those as happening to/for us, but they are a part of an appraisal process. If you can define what that looks like for you, then you may be able to use it more often to get out of a pit, even to retrain your brain to look for that more than focusing on a problem. For this week, you'll be reflecting on positive experiences you've had and your appraisal process to identify how they came about and their impact.

Think of a minor everyday event that turned out really good. How did it happen? What did you do, what was circumstantial, what did someone else do in thought or action?

_____
_____
_____
_____
_____

Think of an occasional event like going out with friends, hiking in the woods, attending a lecture, participating in a group chat where things felt good and easy. What was it about that event or experience that resonated with you? How did you get there?

_____
_____
_____
_____
_____

Big events can be great to fuel dopamine and get neurotransmitters excited. Perhaps it's a friend's wedding, a summer outing, a special date, a vacation, or your favorite holiday. Consider a recent one in your experience, what it was about that event that made it a positive influence for you? For example, did it present an opportunity to see people you care about? Reminisce about old memories? Get out of the house?

_____
_____

_____

_____

_____

_____

_____

_____

_____

_____

_____

_____

_____

_____

_____

_____

_____

_____

When reflecting on these types of experiences, how did you feel? How did the memories affect your mood?

_____

_____

_____

_____

_____

_____

_____

_____

_____

_____

_____

_____

_____

_____

_____

_____

Week 4 ~ Power Tools

If you've ever used a Philips screwdriver to tighten a screw by hand you know that no matter how you torque it, an electric screwdriver can make it seem like you didn't even try. It can be the same way with muddling through a day. We "try" yet things come loose anyway. We set our sights on "Monday" and our expectations of doom follow. We set our sights on "Friday" and anticipation for time off and relaxation follows. It can seem like an endless rollercoaster of ups and downs. There must be something to steady the ship!

Although it's easier to look towards the horizon for rescue, for something to help us power through, for something to change, someone to fix it and make it easier, powering the ship is always the responsibility of whatever engine is on the ship. For you, that is your thoughts, feelings, and actions. If you know how that works within you and what fuels your fire, then you can get in the habit of reaching for the power tools more than focusing on the effort to turn the crank or depend on someone else. You've already done much of the work this month. Now it's time to bottle it up and power up.

Last week you identified events that may be contributors to feeling good or empowered. This week you will be journaling about the most important things you've discovered about yourself the past month to fit those into a process. You'll find some resources included here to review and incorporate as well.

What do you do well?

_____
_____
_____
_____
_____

What do you count as your best accomplishments?

_____
_____
_____
_____
_____

What are some of the key environmental influences that help you feel empowered?

_____
_____
_____
_____
_____

What variables make up your ideal day?

_____
_____
_____
_____
_____

What thoughts make you feel empowered?

_____
_____
_____
_____
_____

Reflect on the 15 questions from week 1 (page 119) which ones helped you the most in identifying your strengths?

_____
_____
_____
_____
_____
_____
_____
_____
_____
_____
_____
_____
_____
_____
_____

In your reflections overall, what can you trust about or count on with yourself to do "right"?

_____
_____
_____
_____
_____
_____

Strength & Attributes

We tend to associate *"strength"* with skills, talents, or things we do well, but they can be so much more. The words we use with ourselves about ourselves can be key and the beliefs that guide us are often tied up in *"born with it or not"*. Whether it's a label someone assigned you or an online self-help resource that determined your personality or other limitations, the onus is on you to decide what your strengths are and will be.

Here is a list of traits and attributes to give you the words that you may want to adopt as your own about yourself, or ones that are representative of strengths that you want to work on cultivating. Circle or highlight those of meaning for you. There may be some cross over with the *Supportive Words* list but worry less about duplication and more about what you can leverage to remind yourself of what the author A. A. Milne expressed through one of his characters, that you are, *"braver than you believe, stronger than you seem, and smarter than you think"*. Powering yourself comes from within; choose healthy words to describe and think of yourself.

Self-Descriptors

A team player	Frugal	My pet(s)
Adaptable / flexible	Generous	Openminded
Agreeable	Good sense of humor / funny	Optimist
Authentic	Handling crises	Patient
Balanced	Hardworking	Persistent
Brave	Helpful	Physically strong
Calm	Honest	Practical
Community Where I Live	Humble	Resilient
Confident	Humor	Resourceful
Creative	Innovative	Responsible
Culture and traditions	Insightful	Self-awareness
Curious	Intelligent	Self-control
Dependable / reliable	Interests or Hobby	Social Connections / Network
Determination	Job, Career Skills	Street smarts
Education or training	Kind and caring	Talents and hobby's
Empathic	Listener	Tenacity
Enthusiastic	Loyal	Thoughtful
Fair	Meditation / Spirituality & Faith	Courteous
Fast learner	Mentally strong	Grateful
Focused	Motivated	Mindful
Forgiving	My Daily Routine	Mature
Friendly	My Family	Independent
	My Friends	Serious

Supportive Words

Circle or highlight the ones that feel good to you:

Accepted	Enthusiastic	Knowledgeable	Restored
Accomplished	Essential	Likeable	Right
Admired	Ethical	Lively	Safe
Adventurous	Euphoric	Lovely	Satisfied
Affectionate	Excited	Lucid	Secure
Agreeable	Exquisite	Lucky	Silly
Amazing	Fabulous	Magnificent	Skilled
Animated	Fair	Marvelous	Soulful
Appealing	Faithful	Masterful	Special
Approved	Fantastic	Meritorious	Spirited
Attractive	Fine	Merry	Strong
Awesome	Fitting	Motivated	Stunning
Beaming	Fortunate	Natural	Successful
Beautiful	Free	Nurturing	Superb
Beneficial	Friendly	Obedient	Supported
Brave	Funny	Okay	Surprised
Brilliant	Generous	One-hundred Percent	Terrific
Bubbly	Gentle	Open	Thankful
Calm	Genuine	Optimistic	Thorough
Celebrated	Giving	Passionate	Transformed
Certain	Glad	Peaceful	Trilled
Charming	Glamorous	Perfect	Thriving
Comfortable	Good	Phenomenal	Trusted
Committed	Gorgeous	Pleasant	Trustworthy
Confident	Grateful	Poised	Unwavering
Consistent	Great	Polished	Upbeat
Content	Handsome	Popular	Upright
Cool	Happy	Positive	Valued
Creative	Harmonious	Powerful	Vibrant
Cute	Healthy	Prepared	Victorious
Dazzling	Heavenly	Pretty	Vital
Dedicated	Honest	Productive	Wealthy
Delighted	Honorable	Protected	Welcomed
Distinguished	Honored	Proud	Well
Divine	Imaginative	Quiet	Whole
Eager	Impressive	Ready	Wholesome
Ecstatic	Independent	Reassured	Willing
Efficient	Innovative	Refreshed	Witty
Empowered	Intuitive	Relaxed	Wonderful
Enchanting	Jolly	Reliable	Worthy
Energetic	Jubilant	Relieved	Zealous
Enough	Kind	Respectable	

Power Prompts

It's hard to believe that how you feel on a good day is still a feeling that exists on a bad day. However, an encouraging word from a friend can change the whole day. Words can solve a problem, give new perspective, and break open possibilities. However, during stress and demand the brain can have a hard time finding anything good to contribute at all because it's so focused on trying to figure out the level of threat by searching all the bad stuff we have stored in memory. Additionally, if there is no one around to navigate the struggle then it is up to you to use your mind to remind yourself of what you know on the good days. Having power prompts can do that for you. Here are some to get you thinking on a positive note and some space to capture the good stuff from the good times and use as a reminder.

I'm good at _____

I feel productive when I _____

I feel strong and empowered when I _____

I'm proud of the way I _____

I did (it) _____ before so I can do it again!

When I think about _____ it makes me happy.

It's temporary, not permanent. This too shall pass.

_____

_____

_____

_____

_____

What's the ideal process for using your strengths?

1. Catch yourself heading down the rabbit hole. Know your internal cognitive and emotional signs when you begin to scan the horizon for rescue. Decide and be determined to look within.

2. Train yourself to reach for your power tools, the notes you have here that can serve as reminders of what your strengths are. They are not all going to work for all situations so be prepared for some trial runs, hits and misses.

3. Use your strengths.
    a. Be brave and stand strong in what you know about yourself that's positive. Do not compare to anyone or anything other than yourself.
    b. Be determined to find what works to empower yourself. Review your list of experiences that empowered and lightened your load then:
        - Think something empowering using supportive words
        - Say something by using your power prompts
        - Do something physically to change your present environmental conditions.
    c. Be smart. Refuse to give up. There are a lot of things that can be true about you, and it is up to you to treat yourself well. Be kind in your mind by minding your words.

"Find what inspires you." – Dr. Vic

July ~ Self-Care

""Be accountable to yourself. Decide on something, set a time, and prioritize it every day. If you can make it to work, school, shopping, or the game, then you can make time to step up for yourself." – Dr. Vic

Self-care can mean different things to each of us, but the primary goal is to care about how you are doing by honoring your needs, values, and leveraging your strengths for a sense of wellbeing. Much of that is motivational and can revolve around what you believe about your effort and potential to impact change.

For example, if you don't believe that eating healthy and exercising will help you get in shape, then the chance that you'll make a concerted effort is slim to none. Especially if results will take some time to achieve and will require self-control. Why? Because your expectations around time and results can dwindle motivation if they aren't appropriately aligned. They can also be complicated by need conflicts involving delayed gratification and patience. If your historical lens of effort has also been tainted with lack of result, the motivation to try again or try something new may be thwarted. You may find yourself more inclined to talk yourself out of doing anything than into doing something. Even shutting out new information and possibilities to avoid further disappointment. Recognizing that cycle and breaking it is going to take work and requires realignment.

The only time you can physically do *"self-care"* is today but setting yourself up for success requires an honest look at yesterday while engaging in reasonable expectations to plan for tomorrow. It can be a tricky balance because the mind wants to get involved by *"thinking and feeling"* beyond the *"physical"*. The result can be internal tension and stress – what if it doesn't work? What will people think? How awful that will feel! Remember "the process" we covered last month? Yes, this is one of the negative ones that can send you down the rabbit hole. Having quick and easy tools that require little *"thinking or feeling"* engagement can help stay the course because they are in fact a form of physical "doing". As long as the mind is under the impression that it's impacting change, whether by thinking or doing, good feelings can follow. Self-care can serve as a power tool in your toolbelt to build resilience and navigate stressors even on the worst days.

This month the focus will be on cause and effect between your effort and choices to obtain the results you want. The main tasks will be to:

1. Inventory and decide on variables that are relevant to you for a sense of wellbeing and what that equates to in caring for yourself.

2. Maintenance. Recognize when you are doing things that are in your best interest even if they don't "*feel*" good in the moment. How well are you doing at "*adulting*" with yourself? Are you better at paying attention to and tending to the needs of your pets, plants, friends, family, and work than yourself?

3. Repair. What to do when things go haywire – what's the prognosis? What do you believe about the challenge? What are you willing to do about it? How can you kick the dust off and move on with what you have left instead of lie in wait for the next shoe to drop?

4. Prevention. Define your baseline of wellbeing to set a sustainable plan for avoiding major break downs.

What does your self-care currently consist of and how do you define it?

_____

_____

_____

_____

_____

_____

_____

_____

_____

_____

_____

_____

_____

_____

_____

_____

_____

_____

_____

_____

Week 1 ~ Feeling Good

"Feeling good" is one of the main measures we use to determine if we're "OK" or not – it's a form of a baseline. That's neither good nor bad or right or wrong but it may not be very useful. At its core, self-care involves layers of needs, values, beliefs, motivation, and strengths that set the bar for your daily activities. Things such as sleep habits, food choices, self-destructive behaviors, relationship dynamics, and even response patterns to stressors and how you recover from them are indicators of self-care wisdom, or lack thereof.

How do we learn self-care? The majority of self-care wisdom and relative habits are learned in childhood and not necessarily by what you did but what others did for, around, or to you. If you were treated with respect and given space to breathe as opposed to press on and toughen up, you are most likely in tune with your mind and body needs. Most likely you were taught by example how to respond in a healthy way and know when and how to refuel self and afford others the same opportunity. However, if you were dismissed and controlled, you may have a tendency to put yourself on the backburner or put high demands on others. You may even question whether you are worthy and deserving when things "feel" out of sorts or bad. The first rule there is to stop trusting those feelings. Obviously, they are not useful. They are left-overs from someone else's inability to *"care"*.

If you have ever had a pet, have children, or had to take care of someone, you know the signs of distress and need even if it isn't verbally expressed. There is body language and facial expressions, even silence can be a form of expression of a need. The same goes for you. Your brain and body is a feedback system that tells you things, but you must be willing to pay attention and listen. Everything matters from the small stuff to the big stuff. Think of it like an engine. If your car throws a belt as tiny and flexible as it may seem in the context of other things, it will make a difference. Your car will go *n-o-w-h-e-r-e* without it.

In that same way self-care has a core curriculum and many electives. According to measures that consider life satisfaction and wellbeing, adequate care for ourselves should result in not only survival but fun, freedom, autonomy, purpose, and belonging. It should in fact, feel good. Additionally, life satisfaction has been found to relate to positive evaluation and perception that things are going in the right direction. Surprisingly, we don't actually need to get everything we want in order to feel that *"things are pretty good"*. Different models outline what the variables are that play a role. For example, according to a positive psychology[2] model the core consists of five domains: positive emotions, engagement, relationships, meaning, and accomplishments. Other models like SAMHSA's[3] *Eight Wellness Dimensions* consist of social, emotional, spiritual, occupational, intellectual, financial, environmental, and physical health. In previous chapters you identified some of these variables, now it's time to operationalize them further starting with an inventory of what you are currently doing and evaluating how that is working for you.

Core Curriculum

Your core is not only what the exercise gurus tell you to work on, it exists in various life applications as well but more specifically are the very basics of what your body and brain need to survive every day. Examples of basic needs that are common to all humans can include:

- *Safety* (mindful travel, avoiding danger, wear seatbelt, car maintenance, clean home environment).
- *Quality sleep* (7+ hours uninterrupted sleep, good sleep hygiene).
- *Balanced/nutritious meals* (vegetables, fruits, grains, antioxidants, proteins, clean water etc.).
- *Physical care* (30+min daily exercise, annual checkups, personal hygiene, intimacy).
- *Relationships/social* (connecting with someone, entertainment, community).
- *Financial health* (manage money effectively, work, pay bills, save some, spend some).
- *Spirituality* (faith, religion, prayer, study, attendance at collective gatherings).

What are you currently doing to take care of yourself in these areas? What are some of the specific things that are meaningful to you in each that are not included here?

_____
_____
_____
_____
_____
_____
_____
_____
_____
_____
_____
_____
_____
_____
_____
_____
_____
_____
_____

It is easy to generalize, justify, or dismiss self-care in the busyness of the day; *"I'm fine"*, *"I ate something"*, or *"I'll survive"*. However, if you are feeling *"off"* or *"tired"* more than you'd like then it's probably time to do a full-on inventory of what is really going on underneath the hood.

This week look for times when you are doing things that support one or more of the basic core areas. Consider your own defining variables from the previous page and list. Here is a tracking table for you to use. Take a few minutes at the end of each day to check in with yourself. Put a checkmark for the self-care areas you tended to *fully* on any given day.

My Self-Care Dashboard

This week I attended to my:	Monday	Tuesday	Wednesday	Thursday	Friday	Saturday	Sunday
Safety, Shelter							
Sleep							
Nutrition							
Physical Health							
Social / Relationships							
Economics / Finances							
Spirituality							

How did you do? Which ones surprised you and which ones did you fall short in doing?

_____
_____
_____
_____
_____

Were there areas that you were doing better in than you thought?

_____
_____
_____
_____
_____

What do you want to change or improve?

_____
_____
_____
_____
_____

Were there areas that you weren't paying attention to or realized what to look for?

_____
_____
_____
_____
_____

Any other observations?

_____
_____
_____
_____
_____

Electives & Preferences

What are your electives? In the previous chapter on *needs* you defined certain *"wants"* and higher-order needs, now is your opportunity to integrate them into your self-care routine.

You know what happens to Jack right? *"All work and no play makes Jack a dull boy"*[4]? That's from the movie *"The Shining"* (not a family flick by the way). It stars Jack Nicholson who plays a father that goes stir crazy when he is only focused on work in isolation. I'm sure you can relate albeit not as brutally but perhaps by feeling of distress at trying to juggle life's many demands, perhaps even your own to-do list.

But seriously, if life is only about survival, work, and meeting demands then you are missing something that is crucial to wellbeing, and you are in fact not taking care of yourself. It is a sure path to ensuring that things will eventually reach a point of feeling out of control, crazy, and even pointless. You must fit some electives in to get off the ventilator and life support and do something that supports *living*!

In previous chapters for Needs, Strengths, and Values you journaled about what is important to you beyond eating and showering, take some time this week to revisit those chapters and make a note of what things you would consider electives:

_____
_____
_____
_____
_____
_____
_____

_____
_____
_____

In the context of your *Self-Care Dashboard*, which ones did you incorporate into your week? Which ones would you like to prioritize more?

_____
_____
_____
_____
_____
_____
_____
_____
_____
_____
_____

Judgement v. Accountability

Another aspect of self-care is judgment versus accountability – one of them sentences you and locks you up while the other provides opportunity for growth. If you don't do what you intend to do, how hard are you on yourself? Were there times that you "*kicked*" yourself during your self-care inventory week?

_____
_____
_____
_____
_____
_____
_____
_____
_____
_____

Accountability in self-care is not synonymous with engaging in criticism and self-defeatism; that will keep you focused on the past, something you can do NOTHING about. Self-care is recognizing your needs and humanness. Nothing is perfect. Even if you don't see others' imperfections, they do exist. Accountability means you remember YOUR goal and keep working towards it rather than getting stuck in comparisons. Giving yourself grace is a part of that and involves what you think, say, and do to and for yourself. Consider your plan in the "strengths" chapter, what can you do to give yourself grace?

_____
_____
_____
_____
_____
_____
_____
_____
_____
_____

What can be your action plan to refocus on what <u>you</u> need in order to care, nurture, self-soothe, support, and encourage yourself when you didn't meet your accountability marks? (If you are finding it difficult to complete this journaling prompt, it may be worthwhile to ask friends or family how they manage it when they fall short of their own measures. You can also search out people to follow on social media who inspire and encourage. The point is to find a way that empowers you independently without putting that responsibility on others).

_____
_____
_____
_____
_____
_____
_____
_____
_____

Of course, there is nothing like feeling supported by people you care about! Who are the people or environmental influences that can trigger positive emotions and motivation for you? Were there any that surfaced this past week during your inventory that are notable?

_____
_____
_____
_____
_____
_____
_____

Week 2 ~ Maintenance

This week the rubber hits the road. So far, you've identified what the very basics are for taking care of yourself which is the equivalent of making sure that you're not feeding your cat dog food and vice versa. What you need is specific and unique to you and being an adult means you're the only one who can take care of you. As I'm sure you have become aware, that can feel like a fulltime job at times. This week the focus will be on addressing the changes you identified from your inventory to make sure that life is not all work and no play, and to find ways to be kind to yourself when things go off track. To nurture and not punish.

One of the things you may have noticed about yourself are the things that keep you on track and those that derail you. For example, some people swear that they can't function without that first cup of coffee in the morning and others can't sleep if they don't have at least thirty minutes of down-time before going to bed. What were the specific things you may have noticed about that one week of inventory? Consider the prompts here and make some notes about your own observations of deal breakers that impede and distract from your ability to take care of yourself each day.

Deal-breakers

If I don't _____ in the morning the whole day is lost.

_____

_____

_____

_____

_____

If I don't _____ before bed, I don't sleep well or I lay awake thinking.

_____

_____

_____

_____

_____

Every day I must _____

_____

_____

_____

_____

_____

If I get myself caught up in _____

_____

_____

_____

_____

_____

I'm easily distracted by:

_____

_____

_____

_____

_____

I often talk myself out of:

_____

_____

_____

_____

_____

I often talk myself into:

_____

_____

_____

_____

_____

What I should do instead:

_____

_____

_____

_____

_____

Readjusting The Sails

In this journal exercise, you will set measurable goals in areas of self-care that you can quickly revisit to gauge your progress. Here are some tips for using the dashboard:

1. The left side section highlights an area of self-care with examples. "*Safety (Safe driving, seatbelt, car care, clean home)*". Being <u>safe</u> may mean something different to you than what the examples show. Use the definitions you set up in week 1.

2. For Target Areas, ask yourself what you wanted to change as identified in your inventory. Choose only 1 or 2 areas to target. Enter those in the fields provided. For example, for the line item "*stressors*" it may involve being mindful of red flags or managing "*triggers*". With "*time management*" it may mean giving yourself more transition time between events. With "*boundaries*" there may be ones you want to set in a relationship. You may want to use a pencil in case you want to adjust things as try some things out and make new discoveries in other chapters.

3. If you don't have changes you want to make in a category, leave it blank.

4. Enter any additional information in the *Notes Field*. Such as current status or baseline, anticipated barriers to tackle, strengths you can leverage, or resources needed.

5. Too many "*to-dos*" can be bad for your health. It is better to focus on one or two things and then as you complete them you can move on to others.

6. Use the S.M.A.R.T. goal strategy from Chapter 1. For example, if you are currently exercising 1 day per week and want to increase to 3 days, set your goal as "3 out of 7 days". (*Specific, measurable, achievable, realistic, and timely*).

7. If you are already successful in one area, make sure to give yourself credit. Enter it and mark it as "COMPLETE" including describing what you are currently doing to make it happen, and why it is "*successful*" to you.

8. Paperclip this section if you think you want to revisit it frequently as a reference and reminder.

Weekly Check-Ins: My Self-Care Dashboard
(See Chapter 3 instructions, chapter 2 goals, and "check-ins")

This week I attended to my:	Monday	Tuesday	Wednesday	Thursday	Friday	Saturday	Sunday
Safety	✓						
Sleep		✓	✓	✓			
Nutrition	✓						
Physical Health	✓						✓
Social / Relationships							
Economics / Finances	✓	✓	✓	✓			
Spirituality							✓
Values		✓	✓				
Needs	✓						✓
Boundaries							
Time Management						✓	✓
Strengths						✓	✓
Stressors				✓	✓	✓	
Goals & Homework				✓	✓		

My Self-Care Dashboard

Areas I want to strengthen and improve
How will I know when I have achieved my goals in these areas?

Safety
(Safe driving, seatbelt, car care, clean home)

Success Measure: __ out of 7 days Complete ☐

Success Measure: __ out of 7 days Complete ☐

Areas I want to target:

Notes:

Sleep
(7+ hours sleep, good sleep hygiene)

Success Measure: __ out of 7 days Complete ☐

Success Measure: __ out of 7 days Complete ☐

Areas I want to target:

Notes:

Nutrition
(Vegetables, fruits, grains, antioxidants, proteins etc.)

Success Measure: __ out of 7 days Complete ☐

Success Measure: __ out of 7 days Complete ☐

Areas I want to target:

Notes:

Physical Health
(Exercise, checkups, personal hygiene, intimacy)

Success Measure: __ out of 7 days Complete ☐

Success Measure: __ out of 7 days Complete ☐

Areas I want to target:

Notes:

Social / Relationships
(Connecting w/someone, entertainment, community)

Success Measure: __ out of 7 days Complete ☐

Success Measure: __ out of 7 days Complete ☐

Areas I want to target:

Notes:

Economics / Finances
(Manage finances, work, pay bills, etc.)

Success Measure: __ out of 7 days Complete ☐

Success Measure: __ out of 7 days Complete ☐

Areas I want to target:

Notes:

Spirituality
(Faith, religion, prayer, study, gatherings)

Success Measure: __ out of 7 days Complete ☐

Success Measure: __ out of 7 days Complete ☐

Areas I want to target:

Notes:

Week 3 ~ Repair and Replace

The ideal self-care is of course prevention, but life is what it is and sometimes things happen that dent, nick, mar, damage, or push you off the edge. During those times you can either repair and replace, drag yourself around wounded and bleeding, or play dead and wait for the end. But feeling good is in your DNA just as much as survival is and while the healing process can feel worse before it feels better, at times even making it seem like things are doomed, it's necessary to go through that in order to know your worth. The only way to learn your true strength is to do hard things. It's the emotional equivalent of weight lifting. To know that you will come out on the other end standing, or slowly making your way back up.

Self-care habits are always a reflection of how you see yourself. It may seem like it's going to be a lot of work to repair the cracks and heal from the pain, but you can do it. You've been through stuff before. Until you decide to press on with determination nothing is going to be easy, and you may get yourself into a habit of avoidance or believing it's not worth it and that can be a death-trap. This all means that you may as well choose the one path that holds the most potential for you to be strong in yourself and feel good. Going through hard stuff whether it's an embarrassment you've experienced or life's mishaps that kill some good vibes, each time you choose to stand up for yourself in your thoughts, mistakes and all, you can feel stronger. It's most often what you believe about a situation that determines prognosis. I'm sure you've heard of the "placebo effect"[5] where an inert substance is presumed to have caused a change in condition even though it has no ability to do so. That can be a power that you use with yourself in self-care by consistent effort, determination, and believing the best.

This week your journal goal is to examine those hard places to build that strength.

"It may be hard but you're worth it". ~ Dr. Vic

When you were little, who did you go to when you got hurt or felt sad?

_____

_____

_____

_____

_____

_____

_____

_____

_____

What did they do that made things better?

_____
_____
_____
_____
_____
_____
_____
_____
_____
_____

What is one of the hardest things you've ever had to face in your distant past that no longer has the same effect as it did at first?

_____
_____
_____
_____
_____
_____
_____
_____

What did you believe about the situation at the time?

_____
_____
_____
_____
_____
_____
_____
_____
_____
_____

What do you believe about the situation now?

_____
_____
_____
_____

_____
_____
_____
_____
_____
_____
_____

Was there anything that made it even worse at the time?

_____
_____
_____
_____
_____
_____
_____
_____
_____
_____
_____

What was it that helped, how did you get through it (time, support, sheer will, other)?

_____
_____
_____
_____
_____
_____
_____
_____
_____
_____
_____

How did you care for yourself and "_self-soothe_"?

_____
_____
_____
_____
_____
_____
_____

What is the most recent event that was difficult for you, how did you recover and who was there for you?

_____
_____
_____
_____
_____
_____
_____

How did you support yourself in terms of self-care or the opposite, what did you find yourself neglecting?

_____
_____
_____
_____
_____
_____
_____

In considering your goals for Self-Care last week, which ones would have helped during those past times of trials and how can you remind yourself of those the next time?

_____
_____
_____
_____
_____
_____
_____
_____
_____
_____
_____
_____
_____

Week 4 ~ Prevention

Who are you responsible for? One of the cornerstones of parenting is to protect our children. If you don't have children, you can think of anything else that is in your purview to take care of. A car, a pet, a family member who's ill, or customers at work. How do you manage it? How do you keep it from harm?

In the case of your pet, you may have a fence around the backyard so a wild animal can't come in and attack it. Your car may be parked in a garage, and you hopefully drive responsibly. Maybe you make sure the family member eats, showers, and takes their medication and at work you listen to your customer's needs, which ultimately protects your job but also prevents them from shopping elsewhere. These are the basic rules of prevention. So why is it so hard to apply them to ourselves? How can we take better responsibility for our own wellbeing?

In this chapter you'll be working on a plan to do just that by leveraging what you've learned so far about feeling good, being productive, and helping your brain feel like it is impacting change. The place to start is with your perception of self-worth. In order to take care of yourself you must first matter to YOU.

List the people or responsibilities that you have on a daily basis besides you. You can reflect on the week 1 inventory or choose a new point that is representative of the average day and week. Include a note of whether that responsibility ultimately impacts your wellbeing or not.

_____
_____
_____
_____
_____
_____
_____
_____
_____
_____

Which ones have no direct impact on your wellbeing and which ones drain your energy?

_____
_____
_____
_____
_____
_____
_____

Which ones are avoidable and unnecessary, why are they and why do you do them?

_____
_____
_____
_____
_____
_____
_____
_____
_____
_____

What should be your focus in order to consider yourself at the top of that list of responsibilities? What should go and what should stay?

_____
_____
_____
_____
_____
_____
_____
_____
_____
_____
_____

If you were to choose three things to remember daily in order to stay well, things that have a trickle-down effect, which ones from your discoveries this month are most important?

1. _____
2. _____
3. _____

Which ones from your Self-Care Inventory need the most attention?

1. _____
2. _____
3. _____

What are three things you can tell yourself as a reminder that you matter?

1. _____
2. _____
3. _____

August ~ Relationships

"When you're suffocating on your own thoughts don't try to be the hero, you'll only tighten the grip. Reach out."
– Dr. Vic

Relating is an unavoidable reality of life, it can also be the most difficult one. We learn how to relate early in life and sometimes the patterns of interaction that the brain adopts is not all that translatable to adult relationships. What to keep and what to discard in terms of outdated perceptions, anticipations, and behaviors is not something most of us have time or the knowledge to decipher and discard. However, how we communicate, interpret, and respond to others is the cornerstone of relating

In this chapter you'll focus on identifying the most important people that play a role in your life. They can be people you really like or those that you feel challenged by (a best friend v. a boss). Be sure to identify which is which in your notes. You'll then be able to explore your interactive patterns and consider areas that you have control over to change. The person's you identify may also become a part of your Self-Care plan to grow a sense of connectedness or to work on setting healthy boundaries to maintain your wellbeing and reduce stress.

The tasks this month are intended to explore:

1. Who you know personally, professionally, in your community, and who you trust.

2. Communication. How is communication working for you in your relationships? Are you more reactive than strategic? What does it mean to *"meet in the middle"* and how do you navigate confrontation and conflict?

3. Relating by design. What's your ideal? Understand your inner circle and dynamics of reciprocity therein. Are you "enough" and authentic or operating by automation?

4. Your needs, their needs, and the give and take of healthy relating. Is what you are doing hurting or helping the relationship?

"When compromise becomes sacrifice it's worth it to get a second opinion." – Dr. Vic

Week 1 ~ Who Do You Know?

    This week reflect on the people you know or that you run into on a daily or weekly basis then write down the ones that have relevance in the areas noted below. You may want to include the reason they are important whether because they have a positive influence or a negative and unavoidable one. Try not to judge whether you want them in your life or not for this exercise.

Personal Relationships (partner/spouse, best friend, parents, siblings, grandparents)

_____
_____
_____
_____
_____

Professional, Work or School Relationships (peers, teachers, coworkers)

_____
_____
_____
_____
_____

Extended Family/Relatives (aunts, uncles, cousins, in-laws ...)

_____
_____
_____
_____
_____

Community Connections (neighbors, agency/organization affiliation)

_____
_____
_____
_____
_____

Online Connections (meaningful networking and regular chats)

_____
_____
_____
_____

New or Recent Friendships / Connections

_____
_____
_____
_____
_____

Person(s) I look up to ...

_____
_____
_____
_____
_____

Others?

_____
_____
_____
_____
_____

In the event of an emergency, I trust the following people:
(Emotional, physical, or other crisis)

- ☐ _____
- ☐ _____
- ☐ _____
- ☐ _____
- ☐ _____
- ☐ _____
- ☐ _____

Any other observations about your current relationships:

_____
_____
_____

Week 2 ~ Communication

Communication has gotten increasingly more complex in the last two decades thanks to the internet and new technologies. The pandemic of 2020 didn't help as most of us probably saw more people online than in person. The problem with virtual interactions is that it gives a limited view that can be deceptive. It also provides limited sensory input during interactions which is something our psyche has relied on since existence began to identify threat.

As a result, we're faced with a whole new set of blind spots that we have simply not evolved enough to process. Seeing someone in person now can be like a slap in the face if it wasn't what we've experienced virtually. For example, sitting in a familiar home environment when meeting with someone is automatically going to feel safer than being out somewhere. The incongruence can leave us questioning ourselves and them between body language, new sensory information, and minor facial expressions overlooked virtually. What we thought we knew may seem different in person.

Additionally, Understanding how you transmit information as well as how you receive and process it is at the core of connecting, building, and maintaining relationships. Although, the extensive variables involved in communication make it impossible to go into the depth it warrants in this book, you can always consult with a professional counselor or psychologist who has expertise relatively. There are also a wealth of books and resources available online. What we will focus on are some areas that you may want to reflect on to be more aware of your patterns of relating, including:

- ✓ Conflict and confrontation
- ✓ Buffer zones & opt-outs
- ✓ Reactivity vs strategy
- ✓ Defenses, games, and collaboration
- ✓ Rules of engagement

Conflict and confrontation

Conflict and confrontation are two of the most common ailments reported by clients regarding their relationships. Someone is afraid to speak their mind for fear of confrontation while the other vomits whatever comes to mind and tries to overtake situations with opinions, or worse, demands. But conflict and confrontation doesn't always show up in those obvious or extreme ways. They can be subtle. For example, someone who was always questioned as a child and feels insecure in their decision-making may feel intimidated if there are too many questions that challenge them. In that way, confrontation is something they define internally vs by common external definitions. The conflict is within rather than outside of because the other person may just be curious but on the receiving end it may touch on a deep nerve that demands defenses go up.

In this journaling prompt, think about your definition and how conflict or confrontation operates in your life and relationships. Is it the extreme or is it subtle? Are you on the receiving end or delivery and controlling end? You can choose any of the relationships you've identified so far whether someone close to you that you avoid conflict with to keep the relationship intact or someone where conflict is unavoidable and frequent.

_____
_____
_____
_____
_____
_____
_____
_____
_____
_____
_____

One of the ways to divert from conflict and confrontation is to be an observer versus a judge to set the record straight. Another way is focusing on the positive and if there is a difficult subject that must be broached, to start on a positive note and be curious rather than presumptive. Doing something new will always take time and practice, in reflecting on the above relationships, what are some areas you'd like to make some changes in ?

_____
_____
_____
_____
_____
_____
_____
_____
_____
_____
_____

Buffer Zones and Opt-Outs

Buffer zones and opt-outs are tools I teach clients to help them create the necessary physical and psychological safety in communication – for self and others. The logic is based on the IT model of download buffering of data and ability to cancel or pause it. These are especially important concepts for people who tend to be conflict averse. It's easy to think of what we want to say when we've planned it out or when it involves something we are intimately knowledgeable about. However, depending on a person's internal variables of experience and disposition, being confronted with new information can serve as a stressor and shut them down. The response then may be less favorable and less intentional, even turning negative and defensive. The aftermath can leave a trail of guilt and second-guessing or turmoil for the relationship.

The Buffer Zone is a space that involves being verbally explicit rather than making assumptions and the Opt-Out provides the tool to do that in a prosocial and pro-relationship way. This is not the same as speaking your mind or being blunt. As a habit of human communication, it's easy to open our mouth and say something rather than think it through. The *"think before you speak"* concept sounds good but is highly impractical, who has time for that?! It is impossible to consider every word that comes out of our mouth or filter every thought we have against prosocial norms and rules. However, if we want to maintain healthy communication that support our relationships, we must find our balance to consider others. For this journal entry take some time to consider your own *"talking"* habits. Do you jump right in, or do you overthink what to say? How do people generally respond when you do partake in a conversation?

_____
_____
_____
_____
_____
_____
_____
_____
_____
_____
_____

What I'm thinking about and what you are thinking about may be on totally opposite ends of a broad spectrum of possibility. This is how it is in all relationships at almost all times of the day. When you get home from work, whatever your brain has been churning on is not what your partner's brain has been focused on, with some rare exceptions. So, when you have something important to tell your friend or partner, what is your process for thinking it through? Are you more worried about what they'll say, what their judgement will be of it or you, and how they'll react, than whether they're ready to receive that information? Consider a recent time when you had something important to say, how did you approach it and what was the response? Did the person respond defensively or were they receptive and supportive?

_____

_____

_____

_____

_____

_____

_____

_____

_____

_____

When we want to meet up with friends we usually ask, "*what do you want to do*?". However, in conversations we don't offer the same choice, we simply jump into a topic that has been on our mind and roll with it leaving the person on the receiving end to fend for themselves. With the Opt-Out concept there is a transition point, a buffer, where you ask permission to "*download*" or if you are on the receiving end, ask for permission to think about it and talk about it at a later time, hit "*pause*".

_____

_____

_____

_____

_____

_____

_____

_____

_____

What could you have done differently?

_____

_____

_____

_____

_____

What do you believe about communication and talking? What rules guide you - "*a right to know*", "a *right to speak*", or something else? How did your family communicate with each other when you grew up? Was it better for children to be seen and not heard or was it each man to himself – speak up or miss out?

_____
_____
_____
_____
_____
_____
_____
_____
_____
_____
_____
_____

How do you step up and speak up for yourself, others, or causes?

_____
_____
_____
_____
_____
_____
_____
_____
_____
_____

Is it important for you to have the last word? How does that affect your relationships and communication? Why do you think that is and do you want to change it?

_____
_____
_____
_____
_____
_____
_____
_____
_____
_____

Reactive v. Strategic

Being reactive versus strategic simply means to act on feelings and emotional upset rather than logic. In this reflection use the Buffer Zone and Opt-Out concept to identify your vulnerabilities. Consider whether you are more inclined to react or think it through and be strategic in your communication. What would you want to change about that and what strategy could you design for yourself based on the Buffer Zone and Opt-Out concepts?

_____
_____
_____
_____
_____
_____
_____
_____
_____
_____

What could you say differently to ask for permission to approach a difficult subject?

_____
_____
_____
_____
_____
_____

What could you say if someone approaches you with a conflict or difficult subject to secure some time to think about it before reacting?

_____
_____
_____
_____
_____
_____
_____
_____
_____

Defenses & Games

In 1964 Eric Berne published a book called "*Games People Play: The Psychology of Human Relationships*". It was a best seller of its time and based on *Transactional Analysis theory* as a means to interpret social interactions. While it may sound a bit "*highschoolish*" to talk about social interactions in terms of games, the brain does use automation to simplify thinking and behavior. If we are accustomed to certain interactions or dynamics in our family that can become a game in the mind that we repeat in other circumstances as well. When someone doesn't know the same dynamic then it can seem like they aren't playing along or in tune with you. As the brain looks for patterns and matches to make sense of how to respond to its environment, the game of relating is either won, lost, or in time-out until those dynamics are resolved. That can be a point of awkwardness and discomfort, even silence. Do you ever feel like you are stuck in a game or a defensive play you didn't even sign up for? How have you been making sense of that and what has been your approach to resolving it?

_____

_____

_____

_____

_____

_____

_____

_____

Some people bring the fun and games to the party, other's keep things together and clean up, then there are the masterminds who sit on a perch of logic and make sure people get home safely; what is your role in your inner circle?

_____

_____

_____

_____

_____

_____

_____

What would you want to change about that if anything?

_____

_____

_____

_____

_____

Collaborative and Common Ground

According to Social Psychology people of differing opinions and views are more likely to put them aside for a high-order common goal. We often refer to this as *"meeting in the middle"* even if it is related to an entirely different topic. It's about finding what there is in common that is worthwhile to both parties and work on that rather than focus on differences. The trick of course is that both parties in fact WANT to make things work. Is this something you have tried before or believe could be useful? If so, define how you would integrate that into your communication strategy by thinking of an example in your existing relationships:

_____
_____
_____
_____
_____
_____
_____
_____
_____
_____
_____

In order to get what I want I usually ...

_____
_____
_____
_____
_____
_____

A more effective approach to work from common goals could be:

_____
_____
_____
_____
_____
_____

Setting Rules of Engagement

In light of what you have explored this week, what could be some of the top rules you want to adopt for engaging in conversation with friends, family, a partner, or coworker to strengthen the relationship?

_____
_____
_____
_____
_____
_____
_____
_____
_____
_____

Any other observations about your patterns of communication in relationships?

_____
_____
_____
_____
_____
_____
_____
_____
_____
_____
_____
_____
_____
_____
_____
_____
_____
_____
_____
_____

*"Never complain without seeking a
solution or being willing to do something about it. It can
become a habit of the mind that keeps you stuck."* – Dr. Vic

Week 3 ~ Relating by Design

We don't often consider our capacity to choose our relationships or even how we relate with others and them with us. We're born and get what we get in terms of family and then later in school we try on different friends and roles to find our place in the crowd. When we enter the workforce as adults there are even more evolutions with twists and turns to adapt and find our place yet again. While relationships may not always be what we'd like them to be and improving communication patterns can help improve them, too often we evaluate them by how we feel or feedback we receive. For this week, reflect on your current relationships and whether you may be measuring them by how you feel or an ideal. What is it that you are looking for that is creating a gap between your current reality?

I want to be treated like ...

_____

_____

_____

_____

_____

Describe your ideal relationship, what do you do / what do they do?

_____

_____

_____

_____

_____

_____

_____

_____

_____

_____

_____

_____

_____

_____

_____

What's the best relationship(s) you've ever had/have, with anyone and why?

_____

_____

_____
_____
_____
_____
_____

My expectations and assumptions usually evolve around:

_____
_____
_____
_____
_____

Whose responsibility is it to keep you happy or to keep others happy?

_____
_____
_____
_____
_____

When you feel unhappy or questioning yourself in the context of your relationships, what do you do? Who do _you_ rely on, if anyone?

_____
_____
_____
_____
_____

Is there someone in your life who relies on you to make them feel better? How does that impact how you feel and/or your relationship when you can't meet that demand and "_fix it_"?

_____
_____
_____
_____
_____
_____
_____

The Comparison Trap - Am I enough?

It is easy to compare to others and what we see online to then arrive at a conclusion or question of whether we're "enough" or not. Now, I've never figured out where the origins of that concept began to have gained such significant ground in people's minds, but it's one of the most common phrases uttered by clients regarding their confidence and presence in the world. It is also the most useless and erroneous thought we can have because "enough" is always dependent on contextual variables. There is no definitive "enough" that even exists. For example, if I have a five-foot ladder that will be enough to reach different places on the wall to hang pictures. However, it won't be enough to reach the gutters on my house to clean them. If we then question whether the ladder is "enough" or not, the only correct answer is "that depends".

The key to defining "enough" is by defining the contexts. Here are some prompts to help you think it through.

What do you compare yourself to? Be honest and reflect on the past week.

_____

_____

_____

_____

_____

How did your comparison points make you feel or think about yourself? How valid are those comparison points; is there information you may not have about that person that would change your perception?

_____

_____

_____

_____

Given the knowledge that you have, experiences you've had, and resources accessible to you, how would you redefine "enough" to be a more accurate reflection of your capacity and potential?

_____

_____

_____

_____

_____

_____

Dr. Glasser used to say that "*all we ever do is the best we can with the information we have at any given time*". Realizing that knowledge is always incomplete is a harsh reality but unavoidably true and accurate at all times. When things go haywire a great question to ask yourself is "*how were you possibly supposed to know that then?*". Accurate comparisons is about perspective and context – it is hard to validate a concept of "*truth*" without those elements.

Given that there are multiple factors at play that are constantly shifting even what you have stored in your memory banks is not always accessible depending on levels of stress, salience, and proximity moment by moment. It can also involve your patterns and habits in response to circumstantial changes, all of which can involve automation and subconscious influences. Every person is as unique as their fingerprint, comparisons with other people is yet another futile endeavor. This is not to give an excuse but there are limitations to brain neurology and functioning. Given those variables, consider things that your mind has been churning on, regretting, feeling guilty about, trying to measure up to because someone else did it, or trying to fix that occurred in the past, how can you reframe that noise to be more reasonable in your judgment – with self and others?

_____
_____
_____
_____
_____
_____
_____
_____
_____
_____

Your Inner Circle

The inner circle of your social network is a place where you can feel safe to be yourself completely. While we tend to define "authenticity" as being ALL of ourselves with others, that is not necessarily the reality, nor is it healthy in all cases. According to the *Johari Window* model we reveal and disclose ourselves differently depending on context and other influences. It's OK not to put all of who you are on display all the time.

For this week reflect on the people you wrote down last week, who is in your inner circle of trust beyond emergency situations that you prefer to socialize with regularly and why? How are you different with them than other people?

_____
_____
_____

_____
_____
_____
_____
_____
_____
_____
_____

If, and when your inner circle gets a new member or one leaves, how do the other members react; what happens? This can be a new baby in the family, a new friend, co-worker, someone gets married, or there is a divorce.

_____
_____
_____
_____
_____
_____
_____
_____
_____
_____
_____

What do you do in times of membership change in your inner circle?

_____
_____
_____
_____
_____
_____
_____

Considering past changes in your life, who has remained steady in the storm for you?

_____
_____
_____
_____
_____
_____
_____

"To heal a wound, you must stop touching it." - Unknown

Week 4 ~ Me, You, Us, Them

With all the daily demands it can be hard to put ourselves in other people's shoes and anticipate their needs or views. However, people in successful healthy relationships tend to make this a priority and a part of relating. It's a process that can help aid the ever important *"give and take"* of relating. If you are constantly the one *"giving"* it can feel one-sided and build resentment which is a definite relationship-killer over time. So, what do you bring to the table and what is in it for you?

In this exercise you'll use the same inventory model that you used with yourself in the chapter on *"needs"*. Select someone close to you and work through the needs template to identify what is relevant for them. You can do this on your own as a reflective journaling exercise or get together and have a conversation about it. This can also be family exercise to collectively explore what your needs are as a family unit.

Who do you select?

_____

Family and/or Partner Basic Needs Inventory

Basic Survival *(safety, food, water, shelter, health etc.)*
Belonging *(love, relatedness, acceptance, caring, culture, language, tradition, identity etc.)*

	Fun *(discovery, learning, adventure, exploring, enjoyment etc.)*
	Power *(competence, meaning, achievement, importance, control etc.)*
	Freedom & Autonomy *(choice, expression of thought/voice, flexibility, creativity etc.)*

Adapted from Dr. William Glasser, 1998, Choice Theory Psychology

Was there anything that surprised you?

_____

_____

_____

_____

_____

_____

_____

Was there anything you can contribute or change to help meet their needs?

_____

_____

_____

_____

_____

_____

Is it hurting or helping?

A relationship is like a child in a family and depending on the number of years in development there will be different levels of maturity. It can take years to build a healthy relationship simply by factor of learning about each other and the underlying footing that it is founded on. Sometimes people come into relationships holding a history of pain and distrust and without even knowing it they continue to reinforce that pattern because that is all they've known. Learning new ways of "*being*" and "*doing*" in relating is a matter of awareness and willingness to make some changes. Part of that is perceptions, communication, and strategy as you've already explored but other ways are more direct by labeling behaviors and choosing something new. The awareness begins with a logic model of what you want from the relationship – the child. Do you want to be closer or maintain a distance? Different behaviors draw in while others push away. So, is what YOU (not the other person) are doing hurting or helping the relationship (the "child")?

In this table there are some contrasting behaviors that you can choose from in a relationship. With the relationships you identified as being either in your inner circle or otherwise important in a positive way, consider what your pattern is and what your ideal is to make new and more effective decisions for relating. These can be a part of your strategy.

Harmful Behaviors	Helping Behaviors
Criticism	Supporting
Blaming	Encouraging
Complaining	Listening
Nagging	Accepting
Threatening	Trusting
Punishing	Respecting
Bribing or reward control	Negotiating differences

Adapted from Dr. William Glasser's Choice Theory, 7 Caring and Harmful Habits.

What are some of your observations and reflections with your own patterns in relating?

_____

_____

_____

_____

_____

_____

_____

_____

_____

What are some of the ways others interact with you that leave you with feelings of discomfort, sadness, frustration, anger, or inadequacy?

_____

_____

_____

_____

_____

_____

_____

_____

_____

_____

_____

_____

_____

_____

What are some of the ways others interact with you that leave you feeling good, supported, encouraged, motivated, or accepted?

_____

_____

_____

_____

_____

_____

_____

_____

_____

_____

_____

_____

_____

_____

_____

September ~ Boundaries

*"You're off the edge of the map mate,
here there be monsters." ~ Captain Barbossa, "Pirates of
the Caribbean"*

A boundary is simply the perimeter that defines something. Like the lines of a picture in a coloring book. You know the picture is a dinosaur because of the lines. Coloring outside of those lines may cause the picture to be skewed or indistinguishable from its surroundings. In other words, the lines protect the integrity of the picture and as long as you want it to be a dinosaur then refraining from coloring outside of those lines is fairly critical.

Similarly in real life, there was a time when the earth was thought to be flat, some still believe that but I'm not judging. At that time, it was also believed that monsters lie beyond its edge and all the rage were those who dared to go beyond those limits. Thankfully an ancient Greek called *"Pythagoras"* theorized that the earth was in fact spherical. Regardless, up until then people's behavior was guided by that perception of a boundary.

Your boundaries operate the same way as physical, emotional, spiritual, and cognitive spaces. You reinforce your boundaries by what you value, believe, think, need, and say or do. Flat or round, you can fear any number of things but like the earth-travelers it can then also keep you hostage because you may never test it out to see if there is indeed a real threat beyond it.

But boundaries are not magical forces that we can't see, they are tangible but only if you know what to look for and pay attention to. Although the hype is all about protecting boundaries by how you *"feel"*, that is probably not the brain-healthiest approach. Don't get me wrong, boundaries should be respected so to keep from harm but the boundaries that are being reinforced today in mental health are not necessarily psychologically healthy ones.

A recent post from NAMI[6] stated that, *"it's ok to unfollow people who trigger you"*. Yes, that makes sense, why follow someone who doesn't add value to your day? However, the principle behind the statement would indicate some ignorance about the negative effects of psychological and behavioral avoidance. To conquer internal challenges like *"triggers"* the best approach according to research is by exposure and extinction, if in fact the circumstances aren't dangerous.

What does all this mean for you? That even though it feels harmful and threatening it may not actually be a present reality. As long as you feed that feeling you are denying yourself an opportunity to break free and neutralize a trauma from memory. *"Triggers"*, as noted in chapter

2 on Stressors, can be cues that allow the brain to retrieve information from memory to make sense of a situation. Healthy boundaries then can mean developing a sense of differentiation and to test adversities to see if they are a present reality or not and break the control of continued false associations and upset.

In this chapter you'll have opportunity to explore your boundaries to map their lines, understand their impact, and set effective and sustainable ways to remove or maintain them that does not involve high-end defenses or armed forces to block, avoid, or attack. Here is a summary of core tasks:

1. Take inventory to map out the limits of your boundaries – physical, cognitive, emotional/feeling, and spiritual.

2. Decision-control processing – is it a true threat and should you do something about it?

3. Speaking up versus acting up – fueling psychological health and prosocial wellbeing.

4. Boundary indicators – setting internal and external red flags.

A Word of Caution

Thinking about the past or difficult experiences can be emotionally exhausting. Some of the prompts in this chapter may bring up difficult memories, thoughts, emotions, or feelings, if you begin to feel compromised or overwhelmed it may be important to reach out to a professional counselor or psychologist who specializes in trauma and boundaries. If you need immediate processing with someone there is a *Crisis and Emergency Resource List* in the last chapter of the book.

Week 1 ~ The Limits of Boundaries

One of the things of concern with the current narrative about boundaries is the notion that they must be protected at all costs under the auspices that it is in the best interest of mental health. Well, that depends on how you define mental health. If the definition is strictly to "*feel good*" then yes, avoid all the hard feels of life and save yourself! However, if you are looking for a healthy psyche that is adaptable, flexible, open minded, free, and resilient that is the worst route to take based on sheer principles of cognitive-behavioral conditioning. If you are guided in thought or action by fears of your own feelings, confrontation, conflict, rejection, or other consequences, that can be limiting. Minding your boundaries is like building up walls to keep things out but unfortunately, that also locks you in and can imprison you. How do you know which is which? Only you can decide that based on your experiences in life, will, resources, dispositions, trauma, and many other variables.

In this weeks' journaling you'll be mapping your own boundaries to recognize where they are, how they protect or inform you, how they may limit your movement in life, and to test out which ones warrant removal versus reinforcement.

Types of Boundaries

Physical boundaries are the most notable ones. Even the law has some critical things to say about how close, when, and what constitutes legal physical proximity, touching, and violation in different contexts (assault, restraining orders, and so on).

In everyday practice, some people are comfortable sitting close to others, they get close to your face when they talk, while others require a lot of space and may pull back. You can see other people setting their boundaries in different ways. At a friendly get-together they may choose the chair that is by the entrance to the room or across from you rather than next to you. Consider your own physical space, if you were to draw a circle on the floor around yourself, how wide would it have to be? When someone approaches you at work, at home, or in a public place, when do you begin to feel confined or uncomfortable? Does the distance vary depending on who and where you are?

___
___
___
___
___
___
___
___

Our life experiences play some role in our preference for physical proximity. For example, if you consider the space that you were given growing up, does that mirror your need for space as an adult? Did you share a room, have no privacy, and what kind of space do you have now for yourself in your home or work? What would you change about that need, if anything?

_____

_____

_____

_____

_____

_____

_____

_____

_____

In some of the current relationships you defined in the previous chapter, are there distinct differences in need for physical space than your own? How do you determine what others' need in order to honor that? Do you ask, observe, or make assumptions? How is that approach working for you?

_____

_____

_____

_____

_____

Cognitive

Boundaries relative to thinking most often show up in the form of fears of "*looking stupid*" and being "*embarrassed*". It can also relate to vulnerabilities like being in unfamiliar situations and meeting new people, knowing what to talk about, or an inability to make predictions about social pecking order. Cognitive boundaries can also relate to opinions, views, experiential differences in knowledge, even intelligence. For example, think about a time when you were at the doctor's office and they rattled off some medical jargon, how competent did you feel? We can cross a boundary by making assumptions instead of asking. Other boundaries may involve reality versus fantasy and distinguishing self from others. We can violate others' boundaries by bringing up topics they are not ready to talk about or hitting someone up for a deep conversation when they are drained from a days' worth of work or study. The brain, like your phone, operates on electrical impulses and there is limit to how much it can process. It is possible to overstimulate cognitions by multitasking and high demand.

Can you identify times when you felt like you were "*braindead*" and someone needed yet one more thing from you? What did you do and how did that impact your mood?

_____
_____
_____
_____
_____
_____
_____

What do you do to protect your cognitive boundaries? In other words, what do you allow yourself to think about or be exposed to? If someone brings up a topic that you know nothing about, is a different view than yours, or that is of sensitive nature, how do you reinforce your boundaries?

_____
_____
_____
_____
_____
_____
_____
_____
_____

Have you ever experienced what seemed like rejection, silence, or opposition from someone else that may have actually been someone else's attempt to protect their boundary?

_____
_____
_____
_____
_____
_____
_____

Positive/Negative Vibes

Feelings are a conscious interpretation of the complex interaction between experiences, thoughts, beliefs, and emotions. Emotions are the explicit signals that the body provides by what the ANS (autonomic nervous system) has been conditioned to react to, good and bad, to establish boundaries of safety. What emotions feel safe to you and which ones compromise or overwhelm you?

_____

_____

_____

_____

_____

Are there emotional expressions of others that are difficult for you to process or be a part of? Like when someone cries or is angry? What emotional boundary does that cross; is it belief related, discomfort because of a need to "fix" things, or something else? What does that boundary violation remind you of?

_____

_____

_____

_____

_____

_____

Finish the next few sentences to see where some of your other boundaries may exist:
I feel compromised and vulnerable when …

_____

_____

_____

_____

_____

I feel uncomfortable when …

_____

_____

_____

_____

_____

When was the last time you experienced a boundary violation? What was happening around you, in your thoughts?

_____

_____

_____

_____

_____

When you recognize you are in an emotionally relevant space, how do you make sense of that – what do you believe about your feelings and emotions?

_____

_____

_____

_____

_____

What are your concerns about your feelings and emotions – I worry that they:

_____

_____

_____

_____

_____

_____

_____

_____

_____

_____

Are there specific emotions that are more problematic than others? Make note of the top three and what you believe they are indicators of or what they mean.

When I feel _____ it means that_____

_____

_____

_____

When I feel _____ it means that_____

_____

_____

_____

_____

When I feel _____ it means that_____
_____
_____
_____

There are many ways emotions can cause havoc, but they can also cause you to feel good like when you see a friend you care about, dog wagging its tail when you get home, a hug, a supportive text, a child reaching for you, a snuggle on the couch, or a warm sunny day. All those are external sensory experiences that remind the ANS that life is good. When there are boundary violations involving negative vibes, it is imperative to restabilize by recharging and finding healthier emotional, cognitive, and physical ground.

I feel best when I think about:

_____
_____
_____
_____
_____

I feel best when I have space to ...

_____
_____
_____
_____
_____

Spiritual

People who have a faith, religion, or a spiritual orientation often talk about a "_knowing_" or experiencing "_signs_" that serve as guides. If that is you, then it's important to pay attention to that part of who you are and what you believe. Boundaries in that way can be relate to sacred scriptures, traditions, rules, even doctrines. If you have spiritual boundaries that are important to you, take some time to reflect and identify what is important to you relative to your faith and where the lines are. What does it look like if someone is close to crossing those lines, what do you do?

_____
_____

_____

_____

_____

_____

_____

_____

_____

Social Boundaries

Identifying boundaries can be difficult in social contexts. It can be easy to get lost in trying to make yourself and others happy, or avoid issues with people we encounter. The list below is based on work by Dr. Jane Bolton[7] and a full version may be available from the author. Read through the questions as points of reflection. Depending on how often and how many of the below items you identify with, it could be an indicator of boundary violations, either by not taking care of your own needs and values or crossing other's boundaries. When thinking through these you may want to place the question in the context of some of the relationships that you mentioned in the previous chapter.

1. Do you feel stressed out, overwhelmed, or burnt out after social interactions?
2. Would you do most anything to avoid hurting others?
3. Do you feel as if your kids (mate, parents, others) run your life?
4. Do you feel as if you are never caught up, or as if your life is not your own?
5. Do you feel taken advantage of by those you love?
6. Do you resent others for being so demanding and inconsiderate?
7. Do others' needs seem much more urgent than yours?
8. Do you see yourself as the only one who can help; therefore, you must say yes?
9. Do you tend to meet others' needs before your own?
10. Do you question the legitimacy of your own needs?
11. Do you hate to disappoint others' expectations?
12. Are you secretly afraid that if you don't do what others ask, they will leave you?
13. Do you say "OK" or say nothing when you would rather not do something for someone, because you don't want a confrontation?
14. Do you deep down believe that if you don't anticipate people's needs and provide services for them, they won't want to be with you?
15. Do you try to convince yourself that your feelings aren't real, that you shouldn't have them, that they don't matter compared to the others' feelings?
16. Are you distressed if one disapproves of you?

17. Are you distressed if someone seems as if they don't like you?

18. If someone criticizes you, do you automatically believe their criticism is true?

19. Do you let other people define what your behavior means? (Ex: *"You don't really love me if you won't..."*)

Any additional observations based on these questions and your answers?

_____
_____
_____
_____
_____
_____
_____
_____
_____
_____
_____
_____
_____
_____
_____
_____
_____
_____
_____
_____
_____
_____
_____
_____
_____
_____
_____
_____
_____

Week 2 ~ Decision-Control Processing

Boundaries hold the power of safety and trust. But reinforcing boundaries can be a challenge, especially with people that we don't want to offend or upset. When we get to a point of deciding enough is enough that's usually a bit too late in the game. We may even have reached a point of resentment. So, how can you make everyday decisions that take boundaries and limits into consideration without catastrophizing or blocking the world? While it can involve a bit of wartime strategizing the key is to understand your controls and indicators. For this week you'll be digging a bit deeper into the various boundaries you explored last week in the context of your relationships. At the end of each day reflect and consider these prompts:

1. Did someone violate your boundaries?
2. Did you violate someone else's?
3. Which ones – physical, cognitive, emotional, spiritual, social?
4. Was it a recurrent or intentional decision to violate the boundary or was it accidental, an isolated incident?
5. Who had the control and what could you have done differently?

Day 1

_____
_____
_____
_____
_____

Day 2

_____
_____
_____
_____
_____

Day 3

_____
_____
_____

Day 4

Day 5

Day 6

Day 7

Week 3 ~ Speaking Up v. Acting Up

Finding the words with others can be a challenge, especially during times of distress and stress. In order to cope we may project, fixate, overcompensate, deny, defend, displace, minimize, and dismiss to protect ourselves from harm. While a common strategy can be to regress to a state of mind that says, "*I don't care*" or "*it's none of their business*" the better option is to leverage verbal communication tools like those buffer zones and opt-outs.

For this week consider the violations you identified last week and ask yourself the same question for each of the same violation category prompts:

✓ "What could you have done last week to speak up instead of act up – whether to ask permission before crossing someone else's boundary or to reinforce your own?". Try to think of the words you could have used to ask permission to cross someone else's boundary or ask that they respect yours.

Physical Boundaries

_____
_____
_____
_____
_____
_____
_____

Cognitive Boundaries

_____
_____
_____
_____
_____
_____
_____

Emotional Boundaries

_____
_____
_____
_____
_____
_____

Spiritual Boundaries

_____
_____
_____
_____
_____
_____
_____

Social Boundaries

_____
_____
_____
_____
_____
_____
_____
_____
_____

Any other observations or thoughts on how to navigate boundaries?

_____
_____
_____
_____
_____
_____
_____
_____
_____
_____
_____
_____
_____
_____
_____

Week 4 ~ Boundary Violations

The ideal scenario is of course to prevent violations to begin with but catching them early enough requires a different analysis. During the past week you journaled about what you could have done differently but knowing when to apply your strategy requires a break down by play and timing. Where is the top of the slippery slope, for you and others?

Choose any of the scenarios from your daily reflections and break them down into a sequence of steps that could in theory be replicated. At which point did you become aware that something was changing for either you, another person, or situation? This can be something as simple as a facial expression or body language, tone of voice, or with modern technology no response to a text or chat message, or a loss of connection. When did things change in the interaction? What did you feel inside or think and what did they say or do before that?

_____

_____

_____

_____

_____

_____

_____

_____

_____

_____

If you were to look for those same signs in the future, which of the steps that you highlighted above could be an early sign of a violation of a relationship rule or your own sense of safety cognitively, emotionally, or physically?

_____

_____

_____

_____

_____

_____

_____

At which point could you have done, said, or thought something different to change your perception or course of events? For example, in week 1 you identified times when you felt *"uncomfortable"*, was that same feeling present during any of your observations of your recent events?

_____
_____
_____
_____
_____
_____

Were there boundary violations that in hindsight you realized posed no real threat, or it wasn't as bad as you had thought? Maybe it felt real, but nothing came of it?

_____
_____
_____
_____
_____
_____
_____
_____
_____
_____
_____
_____

Boundaries consistently crossed within yourself can create a default and habit of the mind by adaptation and desensitization. They can also be indicators of an unintentional pattern and habit that causes incongruence or cognitive dissonance – feeling bad and not knowing why and then projecting onto others bad feelings without a clear target. What are some of your internal red flags that are tell-tale signs that you aren't doing something intentionally according to your needs, values, beliefs, or being authentic?... shooting in the dark?

When I feel _____ it means that_____
_____
_____
_____
_____
_____

When I feel _____ it means that_____

_____

_____

_____

_____

_____

When I feel _____ it means that_____

_____

_____

_____

_____

Extending Boundaries

Are there boundaries that are holding you prisoner? Keeping you from taking the next step in talking with someone, changing what you are doing/thinking/feeling, or limiting your movement in life to consider new opportunities? This is your chance to take the limits off. With each of the categories of boundaries you defined for yourself, reflect on these prompts:

1. How does the boundary keep you safe or maintain to the integrity of who you are?
2. How does it keep you from doing, saying, feeling what you want?
3. What, if anything would you like to see change?

Physical Boundaries

_____

_____

_____

_____

_____

Cognitive Boundaries

_____

_____

_____

_____

_____

Emotional Boundaries

_____
_____
_____
_____

Spiritual Boundaries

_____
_____
_____
_____
_____

Social Boundaries

_____
_____
_____
_____
_____
_____
_____
_____
_____

Any other observations?

_____
_____
_____
_____
_____
_____
_____

If you are finding it difficult to push your boundary limits even a little, then it may be a good time to seek out a coach or counselor to reach new heights.

October ~ Patterns & Habits

"What you know and do is a reflection of what you've been exposed to. You can only do what you know, and online information is not knowledge." – Dr. Vic

Even if you haven't spent time watching a hamster run on its wheel, I'm sure you are all too familiar with the experience. The same view, same routine, going as fast as you can yet ending up no different than yesterday.

We all have different things that keep us spinning our wheels. It can be physical behaviors we always engage in, things we want to do but never do, the way we perceive, interpret, think, and feel can be habitual. The brain feeds on that stuff, matching patterns and routines. Why? Because the brain uses energy, physical, measurable electrical energy, and it's much easier to run the same neurological pathways than having to set up a new route. Exerting energy on new ideas and concepts does require integration into the network of already existing knowledge. The harder to find a place to fit new information, the more resistance there can be. All of which require. That's why most of us do things *"the way they've always been done"*, it's easier, right? Yes, it can be but not necessarily beneficial or healthy.

So, how can you ditch the wheel and train your brain to feel free to do new things, to essentially get control back? The simple answer is to get an awareness of what is keeping you on the wheel to begin with by looking for opportunity to jump off and then having a plan in place to support yourself before, during, and after the jump.

In this chapter we'll explore some of the things that may be keeping you stuck and spinning by revisiting the various concepts covered in the book already. Most of what keeps us on the hamster wheel involves needs, values, beliefs, relationships, and stressors. It's too stressful to do something new, or there isn't enough time. Maybe a friend or relative wouldn't approve if you changed things up. Perhaps your physical body screams when you try to stop, or maybe you believe it means you're a *"quitter"* if you do. It could even challenge old values you've been clinging to. It could even be that staying on the wheel meets a need like having a sense of belonging. For example, *"partying"* in college because everyone does it, or staying in a high-status position for a sense of achievement and competence at the sacrifice of time with family. So, what do you do? You keep running the wheel to avoid rocking the boat.

The good news is that even though you may get some bruises when jumping off the wheel, and it may feel bad or awkward for a while, you will heal and recover. It's an inescapable neurological reality, but everyone's timeline differs and that's where things can get tricky. If it takes too long. But All those things that keep you stuck can get reorganized in your brain to work for you rather than you being a slave to them.

The prompts in the coming pages are designed to help you examine some of your habits and patterns. Those that aren't serving you and identify new ones that are more in line with your ideal for quality of life and life satisfaction (values, beliefs, and needs). The tasks for this month explore:

1. Your wheel of monotony and ways it may not be getting you where you want to be.

2. Cognitive habits and patterns that can keep you stuck by automation and things that fall below your radar.

3. Your routines through a lens of historical experiences, defaults, go-to's, familial influences, and adopted patterns of coping.

4. How to set your sights. To decide what's in or out and establish more intentional patterns and habits that serve your true values, needs, beliefs, and goals.

Week 1 ~ My Wheel

What does your wheel look like and what keeps you on it? Over the course of this week start to look for habits and patterns in the way you think, perceive of, and respond to people, places, things, situations, and events. What is their influence on your day when they surface? Then at the end of the day reflect and make a note of them. There is also a section to write down your explicit habits and identify how they serve or impair your ability to move freely in life. Here are some other prompts to fuel your exploration.

Patterns

I always _____

_____

_____

_____

_____

I never _____

_____

_____

_____

_____

_____

In conversations with people, I tend to _____

_____

_____

_____

_____

_____

When I see _____ I usually _____

_____

_____

_____

_____

_____

I can't stand it when _____

_____

_____

_____
_____
_____
_____

I always wish that _____
_____
_____
_____
_____
_____

If only _____
_____
_____
_____
_____
_____

Things that keep me going are _____
_____
_____
_____
_____
_____

Is there someone close to you that has ever mentioned or complained about a habit/pattern you have?

_____
_____
_____
_____
_____
_____
_____
_____
_____
_____
_____

Explicit Habits

Some common habits that can keep people on the hamster wheel simply by neurological engagement of powerful hormones and neurotransmitters include:

Over-eating	Social media use	Internet searching
Smoking (tobacco/marijuana)	Alcohol	Gaming
Binge watching (YouTube/TV)	Staying up/eating late at night	Drug use or pain killers

Some of these can be quite serious and even health-threatening if stopped abruptly or with chronic use, like alcohol and pain killers. Although, we like to categorize these in terms of *"addiction or abuse"* I rarely find that useful. What I do find useful is to identify how they operate in someone's life and what purpose do they serve.

What was your motive when you began the habit? Was it intentional or accidental?

_____

_____

_____

_____

_____

How did it feel and what did you think about it then? What do you think and feel about it now?

_____

_____

_____

_____

_____

I'm sure you've tried to give up and/or change these or other habits only to encounter an internal army of resistance. Part of the problem can be external life demands that max you out. Thinking about self-control, pain of *"withdrawal"*, setting a plan in place, or how much work it will be is like one more demand to put you over the edge. Easier to just keep feeding the beast. Additionally, the time to break a habit can be significantly longer than starting one when it involves both physically and psychologically engaging substances. Today's fast-paced ways don't easily afford the luxury to stop and focus on what you need in order to overcome it. The time, effort, and even cost is sometimes not within reach.

For the most serious levels of habits (addictions) it may even require some degree of hospitalization and medical attention and regular meetings for support and accountability to serve as a reminder while the brain does a re-set to establish new neurological connections. Often that can involve prolonged discomfort which means that you must want something different *more than* to soothe the ache while you are in transition. It can start by reevaluating those *"wants"* against what *"is"*. For a time, the brain may be extremely displeased and serve up lies and information to your mind that says, *"it will never work"*, *"you're too far gone"*, or *"must have it!"*. With all this at play, it may seem impossible which is why some don't even try. The key is to not give up until you find what works for you and to do that long enough to override the brain with your mind.

So, what are the things that trip you up and make you stay or return to the hamster wheel?

Physical symptoms and demand? When I feel _____
then I know I must _____

_____
_____
_____
_____
_____
_____
_____
_____

Cognitive symptoms and demands? When my mind starts to _____
then I know I must _____

_____
_____
_____
_____
_____
_____
_____
_____

Emotional/Feelings of discomfort? When I feel _____
then I know I must _____

_____
_____
_____
_____
_____
_____
_____
_____

What does your habit align with and how? Is it meeting a need for belonging, freedom, or something else? You may want to revisit your journal entries from the respective months to see if your reflections have changed or stayed the same.

Needs

My _____ habit meets my need for _____

_____

_____

My _____ habit conflicts with my need for _____

_____

_____

_____

_____

_____

Values

My _____ habit is important to me because _____

_____

_____

My _____ habit conflicts with my _____ value

_____

_____

_____

_____

_____

Beliefs

My _____ habit is important to me because I believe that if I stop

then _____

_____

_____

My _____ habit conflicts with my belief that _____

_____

_____

_____

_____

_____

Consider what you identified in your goals week 1 of January, is there a habit or pattern that interferes with any of your goals? What would you like to see change?

_____
_____
_____
_____
_____
_____
_____
_____
_____
_____
_____
_____
_____
_____

If you were to have a friend with the same dilemma, what would you advise them to do? What plan could they put in place that you would consider yourself?

_____
_____
_____
_____
_____
_____
_____
_____
_____
_____
_____
_____
_____
_____
_____
_____
_____
_____

Week 2 ~ What Were You Thinking?!

Most of what we think up until we're around age 25 comes from what we were *"grown on"*. In my experience, those who seek counseling around that span of transition (17-27) into adulthood report feeling like the ground has been pulled out from under them, like nothing makes sense, or as if surfacing from a coma. What's going on?

The gist comes down to the conflict of two major life transitions occurring at the same time: the brain's connectivity development concluding while also being faced with a new world of freedom and responsibility. Now, science has yet to explore and consider this but the reality of the stress-conflict can be great and unfortunately as in most desperate situations, the brain turns inward to whatever dialogue and dynamic existed throughout youth (the past).

Adulthood involves many trials and errors the first few years. The new high demand situation of *"adulting"* means that the brain turns to automation and internal habits without you (the mind) knowing it. Whether you grew up with supportive or dissenting and critical voices, those can speak more loudly than ever during this time. When things do go wrong, and they will, you then make automated assumptions based on faulty foundations being served up by your brain. You may believe the worst, question every move, believe everything is your fault, or that you aren't enough.

Why? Before you even enter your teens, your habits and patterns are set for you. Your brain is so new that it can't comprehend, reason, or understand most of what happens until you are well into your teens. Additionally, before your teens you have a natural developmental stage where you aren't able to differentiate between others and yourself. Whatever they are doing or suffering you may adopt as your own feeling and discord. Parents divorcing, fighting, dysfunction at home, or other issues, you may attribute to something you did.

While you may not remember the details of experiences, the feelings and paired association with events and self-blame remain. Subsequently that pattern of feeling and thinking may also remain and resurface by automation when things go wrong in early adulthood. There is a neurological reality that can't be ignored here, the brain simply has nothing else to deliver to your mind.

So, what are the psychological phenomena that can continue to fuel learned cognitive habits of exposure outside of your awareness? In this section I've listed the ones that tend to resonate most with clients to explain *why they do what they do* and to find their levels of control. These may take a bit longer than a week to explore so you may want to paperclip this section for continued reflection in the future.

Mere Exposure Effect

According to Lazarus[8] The *Mere Exposure Effect* is a result of something entering an individual's realm of perception (a condition or stimulus) that then influences their attitude towards it. It doesn't even have to be within their awareness, like the "*banner*" experiment story I shared in the Introduction of this book. The stimulus or condition can be anything, and it can activate any number of feelings, thoughts, or patterns of behavior that you have stored in your brain's network. This does <u>not</u> mean that you can be "*controlled*" by what you see and experience, but your control mechanism can fall outside of your present realm of access. This means that when you feel "*off*" or can't identify a reason for the way you are feeling, thinking, or reacting, it may be worth questioning what you may have come into contact with by retracing your steps.

If you consider today, what can you identify that you have been exposed to via technology and/or in person? Products, values, beliefs, opinions, other advertisements, someone else's bad mood or attitude, searching health information online?

_____

_____

_____

_____

_____

What are some of the "*sponsored*" things you've seen?

_____

_____

_____

_____

While being online do you recall seeing any pop ups or sidebar movements but don't recall what was in them? What were you doing at the time and what did you notice? Did you notice any changes in your thoughts, mood, attitudes, or motivation after being online?

_____

_____

_____

_____

_____

Time and Space Associations

Paired associations[9] are the sneakiest of psychological phenomenon if you don't know what to look for. The concept is affiliated with *Behaviorism* similar to Pavlov's dogs[10] and *classical conditioning* which is simply two things occurring at the same time to produce a reaction – emotional and/or behavioral. For example, when you smell cookies baking what does your brain tell you? After you watch a scary movie, do you flinch and question every shadow? Do you ever find your mouth watering at the thought of, or seeing, a grilled steak? That is a paired association. Your brain and mind have learned that cookies and steak are tasty, pleasant, and fulfilling. By contrast, your brain also knows that whatever happened to those people in that scary movie was associated with darkness, weird noises, and bad outcomes. When faced with those same situations the brain then responds accordingly by evoking feelings, thoughts, and behaviors respectively. You don't have to think about them to make them occur.

This is what can happen with everyday events that occur with any frequency when you aren't paying attention. For example, perhaps you always think the worst when you are stuck in traffic. Before you know it, you dread traffic and you're telling everyone how bad your day will be if you get stuck in traffic again. All the while you could pair that experience with something else, like an opportunity to listen to some fun music and sing your heart out. In this journaling experience try to consider your everyday experiences and how they may be paired with thoughts, feelings, and reactions/behaviors. Here is an example of a process you can consider:

In the morning my paired associations are:

When I do or see _____

I think and feel _____

Are those automated or intentional?

_____

_____

_____

What are some optional interpretations or meanings?

_____

_____

_____

What are some things you could do to pair up new associations between interpretations, thoughts, and/or actions and situations?

_____

_____

_____

_____

_____

_____

_____

_____

_____

_____

What other scenarios are paired associations in your day-to-day experiences?

_____

_____

_____

_____

_____

_____

_____

_____

_____

_____

_____

A paired association we don't often think about is the *time-space* variable. However, the brain-mind-body system is rhythmical and pairs seasons, time of day, and light changes with sensory information and cognitive structures to create *Schemas*[11]. For example, maybe you have a habit of changing out your wardrobe from summer clothes to winter ones when the cold of fall sets in. You don't even need to put it in your calendar, the cues are all around you. The changing of the leaves, needing a jacket, and the chill when you start your car in the morning all remind you. It can also be a schema about *Mondays* or "*bad weather*". Most people dread Mondays and when I say I love them, they question my sanity, why? It's a mismatch with the schema they have about Mondays. In Sweden we have a saying that "*there is no such thing as bad weather, only bad clothing*" so when I say I love storms, cloudy days, and snow, I'm met with the same response. The time-space is important to consider. We pair time and environment with perceptions that can lock us into patterns of thinking that may have other options. What are some of the schemas in your life that relate to places and spaces and lead to assumptions or expectations?

_____

_____

_____
_____
_____
_____
_____
_____
_____
_____
_____
_____
_____
_____
_____

Environmental Contamination

A similar concept to paired association is *State-Dependent Learning*[12]. It is also a danger-zone because it can cause the brain to fall prey to what I refer to as "*environmental contamination*". State-Dependent Learning can be something as simple as sitting in the same spot doing the same thing on a regular basis. Like the student remembering their homework when they take their seat in the classroom but not so much the night before when they were out with friends. It can also be studying while listening to classical music. In the future, whatever was studied will be easier to recall when the person is in that same space of experience again.

Unfortunately, this applies to difficult thinking too. If you always sit in that favorite chair and tell your best friend about life's problems, there is an association made. Perhaps you have a crappy boss and all the way home from work every day you think about that. You're making it much easier for the brain to serve up that same information due to those cues. The problem is that even when you head out on an exciting road trip with your partner or family, you may feel drawn to remember and talk about the boss issues rather than being in the moment. But the worst habit most of us tend to engage in is getting into bed and laying there thinking about problems or worries. All we are doing is teaching our brain that it's ok to do that "*thinking*" activity in that space and time not realizing that it is making it much easier to keep doing it.

Recognizing the learned experienced between where you are and what you think about can help you be more conscious as to where you allow your mind to be in various spaces.

What types of patterns do these scenarios bring to mind for you that could be impairing your ability to feel good in your own home and space?

_____
_____

_____

_____

_____

_____

_____

_____

_____

_____

_____

_____

Attribution Errors and Biases

When you have paired associations that are negative in nature and that occur in a routine pattern, there are things that can reinforce those that can complicate the ability to make changes. The more common ones are *attribution errors*[13] and underlying *biases*[14] which is really just how you make sense of the resulting reactions, feelings, thoughts, or other behaviors in yourself or with others. What does it mean? Is it an automated and learned response or is it something pathological? For example, if your best friend who always texts you back right away stops doing so, what are you more inclined to think?

   a. The relationship is on the rocks
   b. She's super busy
   c. You did something wrong
   d. Other? _____

Whichever one you chose, that choice has its roots in what your biases are and therefore what you attribute her behavior and your internal response to. If you are secure in how you treat her, your prior relationship interactions or history, and you happen to know she has had to take on extra projects at work, then you may be fine.

However, if you come from a family dynamic of everyone being manipulative or punitive you may think otherwise and either internalize the problem or place blame elsewhere – catastrophizing rather than reaching out and asking her if *"everything is ok, haven't heard from you like I usually do"*. What other scenarios like this one do you experience with any frequency where your mind spins on possible issues and worries?

_____

_____

_____

_____

_____

_____

_____

_____

_____

_____

_____

_____

_____

_____

_____

_____

What do you usually think it means? Are there any automatic assumptions you are making? (You can also revisit your journal notes on *Beliefs and Motivation* for insights on past reflections).

_____

_____

_____

_____

_____

In terms of paired associations and how you make meaning of daily events, there is always a choice. A saying I like to hang my hat on as a reminder is to:

> *"Be careful what you allow your mind to settle on and allow into long-term memory for later use and interpretation. You can't delete a memory". – Dr. Vic*

Those paired associations and biases can play tricks. The only way to overcome them is to recognize when you are drawing conclusions without thinking so to question the facts and seek out objective reasoning. To develop new intentional attributions and override those old biases.

Priming and Appraisal

Priming is a process of exposure that cues up stored information from the brain. For example, it's the car or time of day in the case of thinking about that crappy boss or the comfy chair that reminds you to call your friend because you just *"gotta tell her about _____ !!!"*.

It's a re-exposure that creates salience in thinking, doing, and feeling. It's also probably the most complicated of psychological phenomena, especially in cases of PTSD (*Post-Traumatic*

Stress Disorder) because just like the mere exposure effect, it can have influence below a person's radar. Additionally, it can deliver dire emotional consequences if a person is not able to resolve the conflict with a reasonable explanation – *"why am I feeling this way?"*. This is where *Appraisal* can help once an *association* is identified.

Appraisal can be an automated or intentional subjective interpretation of what is going on at any given time by a person. It is the meaning-making process we use. It's essentially what you've been doing by journaling in this book. You've broken things down and examined them to understand them by cause and effect.

For this journaling exercise you'll be doing that specifically to try to identify those instances in your day-to-day where there may be a primer present. What things do you do in your mind that you don't even think about or question? Consider when you open your eyes in the morning, what is the first thing you see, think, and/or do? Have you ever questioned it or tried to do something different?

_____

_____

_____

_____

_____

When you see certain people? What do you automatically think?

_____

_____

_____

_____

_____

What is your process of appraisal, and does it vary more by situations and/or your internal feelings?

_____

_____

_____

_____

_____

What are some things that tend to *"prime"* you to think, feel, and do something by automation? Maybe you get in a bad mood when your boss yells at you? Did you know you can choose to be in a different mood despite those outside forces? You may want to revisit your notes from February and week 3 on Triggers.

Where could you take action in your mind or otherwise to "*appraise*" it differently?

_____

_____

_____

_____

_____

_____

Proximity

Proximity is not necessarily an official psychological phenomenon but does have roots in *Gestalt Psychology* and perceptual organization. There is a physical reality behind how the mind and memory operate. The closer you are to something the more real it will feel. For example, if you have ever had a bad break-up and it was all you could think about, with every thought it probably felt fairly fresh and real. But with the passing of time and reduced proximity in thought and reality, the easier it was to move on.

Similar to "*priming*", proximity can serve as a cue where most recent events are more salient and accessible for recall than past ones. This is why crime investigations insist on interviewing witnesses as close in time of the incident as possible. The memory can undergo reorganization and shift things around with the passing of time and new experiences. Once that reorganization has taken place the proximity variable can be altered by mere thinking, and its impact reduced to allow more self-awareness and control. Proximity can include words, places or scenery, situations, people, even things you "*follow*" online.

Are there influences in your life that involve habits or patterns fueled by simple proximity – being "*too close for comfort*"? What if anything could or do you want to change about that to gain more control? How long do you think you'd need to make a change? What resources do you need to secure?

_____

_____

_____

_____

_____

_____

_____

_____

_____

_____

Cognitive Archeology

What are the foundations of your brain? Beyond genetics and neurology, your mind has been accumulating and storing up information for as long as it has existed. One of the ways to understand yourself is to dig into that networked history by looking at the narrative that shaped you. The *Life Script*[15] format can help you do that.

With this journaling exercise you can choose several days to complete this or in one sitting. Based on principles of psychological exposure and priming you may find that over time, new revelations about your past may surface as these play out over different experiences in the coming weeks. You may even want to talk to your family about some of their perspectives and recollections as well.

Try to be as specific as possible, like telling a story. For example, if your mother always told you to be good, what did she expect you to do to demonstrate that you were good (who said or did what and when)? What was that like for you? What did others say about it or how were your siblings treated differently? These are all influences that, in some way, contributed to how you think about things today. They may even hold secrets to ruminations you have or ways you see the world.

1. Which parent named you?

2. What is the story about your birth?

3. How would you describe yourself and how do others describe you?

4. What situations or behaviors led your mother to compliment you?

5. What did your mother say when you did something wrong or disappointed her?

6. What types of advice did your mother or father/other parent give you?

7. What situations or behaviors led your father or other parent to compliment you?

8. What did your father/other parent say when you did something wrong/disappointed them?

9. What body language or facial expressions did your parent(s) use to indicate that you did something wrong or show their disappointment?

10. What types of advice did other family/relatives give you?

11. What were the family rules (relatives/grandma/grandpa/uncles/aunts)?

12. What were the family secrets?

13. What nicknames have people called you? What do those mean?

14. What kind of person did you want to be when you grew up?

15. What kind of person did your parents want you to be?

16. What do you like most about yourself?

17. What do you like the least?

18. What bad feelings have you had most in your life?

19. When did you first realize these feelings? Give an example of an incident with details.

20. As a child what situations led you to feel that way?

21. In what situations do you experience this now?

22. In what ways do you take out your bad feelings on others?

23. What situations do you have trouble dealing with?

24. What people do you have trouble dealing with?

25. What do people say about you?

26. How do you handle these?

27. What do you do afterwards?

28. What feelings were permitted or not permitted in your family?

29. Who worked in your family when you were growing up?

30. Who had control of and managed the money and paid the bills?

31. What is the highest level of education of your parents? Your grandparents?

32. What was your favorite story as a child (book, tv, radio program...)?

33. If everything goes wrong, what will you be doing in 5 years?

34. If everything goes right, what will you be doing in 5 years?

35. What events will be milestones in your life?

36. What will you be free to do after that?

37. What do you want written on your gravestone?

38. What do other say about you?

39. What are your greatest fears in life?

40. What do you wish your mother would have done differently in raising you?

41. What do you wish your father/other parent would have done differently?

42. If by magic you could change anything about yourself or your life, what would it be?

43. How do you think counseling will turn out for you?

44. If your life was a movie, what kind would it be?

45. Why do you think things happened the way they have in your life?

Any other observations or discoveries you want to make a note of?

_____
_____
_____
_____
_____
_____
_____
_____
_____
_____
_____
_____
_____
_____
_____
_____
_____
_____
_____
_____
_____
_____
_____
_____
_____
_____
_____
_____
_____
_____

Week 3 ~ Automation & Routine

Given all that you have now explored relative to psychological phenomena that have the potential to influence your day-to-day experiences, take some time for a week and observe yourself and see how those play out in real-time. Use the concepts introduced from last week as a lens for what you think, feel, and do. Begin by documenting your baseline and what your typical day or routine is. Include work, social life, social media, internet use, eating, hobbies, or other things you don't really have to think too much about and still do.

Morning

_____
_____
_____
_____
_____
_____
_____

Daytime

_____
_____
_____
_____
_____
_____
_____

Evening

_____
_____
_____
_____
_____
_____
_____

Day 1

_____
_____
_____
_____
_____
_____
_____

Day 2

_____
_____
_____
_____
_____
_____
_____

Day 3

_____
_____
_____
_____
_____
_____
_____

Day 4

_____
_____
_____
_____
_____
_____
_____

Day 5

_____

_____
_____
_____
_____
_____
_____
_____

Day 6

_____
_____
_____
_____
_____

Day 7

_____
_____
_____
_____
_____
_____
_____

What stands out to you the past week the most?

_____
_____
_____
_____

Which psychological phenomenon did you find yourself using or subject to the most?

_____
_____
_____
_____
_____

What, is your most frequent pattern of response to external events?

_____
_____
_____
_____
_____
_____
_____
_____
_____
_____
_____

Where did you have the most control in your routine – morning, daytime, or evening?

_____
_____
_____
_____
_____
_____
_____
_____
_____
_____
_____

Anything you'd like to change?

_____
_____
_____
_____
_____
_____
_____
_____
_____
_____
_____

Week 4 ~ Defaults and Go-To's

This month you have explored the habits of your mind, actions, and life patterns. I suspect like most of us there are things you'd like to change to live life in a more fulfilling and authentic way. All change begins with awareness and requires a move beyond focusing on the bad to focusing on how to be the change in your own life and setting an action plan in motion that is sustainable. Two things to look for beyond psychological phenomena are your hardwired *defaults* and *go-to* responses. According to research[16], ANS fear responses can be activated outside of your awareness in less than 1/20th of a second and can take ½ a second within conscious processing. Like with the banner experiment and four-second rule of creating familiarity it's easy to see how early life events can have a grave impact by exposure and associations. It also leaves room to question what you are thinking, believing, and doing on a regular basis – is it you or something from the past? Here are some journaling exercises to flush some of that out and set a plan of action.

Defaults

Defaults are typically those things that are "*hardwired*" based on a personal history of experiences, relative responses, and feedback. It can be a vicious cycle depending on how many people and things in your everyday life serve as reinforcers or that are similar. The most prominent of defaults can be found in your thoughts and perceptions. It can be like an internal judge and critic that tells you what is ok and whether you're not ok. For most of us we simply follow the voice passively and believe whatever it dishes out.

Consider your notes this month: your wheel, thoughts and experiences in week 2, and your automated responses and routines then go through the table of *Rules and Messages* to see if there are any that may have played a role. The table hosts various negative behaviors and "*unspoken*" rules that have the potential to translate and contribute to a negative internal voice from childhood into adulthood by *conditioning*[17]. This is in contrast to the human natural tendency to *trust* and feel secured provided there is a healthy supportive environment. These messages and roles tend to have the opposite effect and leave negative emotional marks.

Negative Feedback / Behaviors	Negative Messages and Rules
Shaming Humiliating Degrading Disgracing	▪ Don't express your feelings, get angry, or cry ▪ Always be in control ▪ Change is bad, maintain status quo ▪ Shame on you! ▪ Look at your brother, he doesn't do that!
Criticizing Disapproving	▪ Be good, nice, perfect ▪ Always look good

Negative Feedback / Behaviors	Negative Messages and Rules
Joking about Teasing Laughing "at"	▪ Avoid conflict / dealing with it ▪ I wish I'd never had you ▪ Do well in school ▪ Be a "man"
Manipulating Controlling Overpowering Bullying	▪ Don't ask questions ▪ Don't think or talk, just follow directions ▪ How can you do this to me?!
Deceiving Tricking Discrediting Set up for failure by vague demands	▪ Making negative light of feelings, wants, or needs ▪ Do as I say not as I do ▪ You can't get anything right ▪ That's not true ▪ Only "bad" people do that!
Betraying Discrediting	▪ Be seen, not heard ▪ You caused it ▪ Don't discuss the family with outsiders: keep the family secrets ▪ Don't betray the family ▪ You owe it to us
Intimidating Hurting Being cruel Threatening Inflicting fear	▪ Don't talk back ▪ Breaking promises ▪ Don't contradict me ▪ Raising hopes falsely
Belittling Patronize	▪ You should be better or different ▪ You're so stupid or bad ▪ *If only* you were better or different ▪ I'm always right and you're always wrong
Limiting Stifling	▪ Big boys don't cry ▪ Act like a nice girl (lady) ▪ We won't love you if you… ▪ Your needs are not all right with me ▪ You'll never accomplish anything, amount to anything
Misleading Withdrawing emotionally Withholding love Responding inconsistently	▪ You're so selfish ▪ You're driving me crazy ▪ Hurry up and grow up ▪ Of course, we love you… ▪ Do as I say not as I do ▪ You did this to yourself
Dismissing Minimizing Guilting Invalidating Not taken seriously	▪ You'll be the death of me yet ▪ Don't cry ▪ I'm sacrificing just for you ▪ You're not good enough ▪ Because of you… ▪ You don't really feel that way ▪ Don't be like "that" ▪ It didn't really hurt

Adapted from Charles Whitfield, M.D. 1987, Healing the Child Within.

Any other observations about these rules and messages? Which ones look familiar? What is a story you can tell about how you learned the message or rule? In the past week, what was your opinion, rules, or a *"dictate"* that may be a sign of one lingering from the past?

_____

_____

_____

_____

_____

_____

_____

_____

_____

_____

_____

_____

_____

Go-to's

Go-To's are your responses to external and internal feedback: what you have told yourself in different situations and what others have said or done to you that influenced you to adopt a behavior or perception. They often involve coping mechanisms. For this exercise take some time to consider the examples in the table and see if you can identify anything familiar about them, maybe something you've observed in how your parents, siblings, grandparents, or aunts or uncles deal with situations in their life and maybe even you.

Defense	Minimally Effective / Maladaptive (Purpose / Examples)	What I want to do instead …
Compensation	This can be a healthy defense when used to highlight accomplishments and positive attributes. However, it can be maladaptive when it is used to *overachieve* and mask a perceived weakness. It can be the person who has a pattern of staying late at work and takes on more work than what is needed, or reasonable, for recognition. This can be a defense involved in imposter "*syndrome*" experiences. It can also be the teenager who perceive themself to be less than others and, in an attempt, to "*prove*" themselves bring attention to areas they think make up for the deficit according to sociocultural norms. This can all lead to burnout.	
Denial	Denial can be an attempt to normalize something rather than deal with it. An elderly man who can't hear what his wife says yet claims he doesn't need a hearing aid because she just talks too softly anyway. The college student who goes out partying and binge drinks every weekend and says, "everybody does it".	

Defense	Minimally Effective / Maladaptive (Purpose / Examples)	What I want to do instead …
Displacement	Displacement is an effort to find a safe target to let out negative or unacceptable energy, even aggression. Ideally to express oneself where there will be the least potential for repercussion. Like *Reaction Formation* this is a form of concealment of a true internal impulse. It can be the man who lacks authority and power at work, so he goes home and bosses the wife and kids around. It can be the teenager who doesn't have a voice or control at home/school who instead stuffs it down with food, drugs, or overshares every opinion and thought on social media.	
Fixation	Fixations are attempts to remain in a life stage or state that is comfortable and non-threatening. Freud defined these in terms of anal or oral fixations and stages that a child may get "stuck" in if they struggled to master a developmental task or had an unmet need. For example, trouble weaning off the bottle may later translate to nail-biting. Strict versus relaxed methods of potty training may lead to obsessively organized individualized versus messy ones. Within basic psychological terms this is simply an obsessive preoccupation or a secured habit to maintain control. It can be the person who starts a new job and struggles with self-esteem or social situations. In order to maintain comfort, they may fixate on keeping busy or overwork to avoid having to go to lunch with peers or attend special events. People worried about verbal confrontation may talk excessively. Fixation can be a feeling of emptiness that becomes an obsession to fill or an addiction to self-soothe.	
Identification	The Identification defense involves a person trying to create a positive association between self and successful organizations, people, or activities. The purpose is similar to introjection and compensation as in establishing an affiliated positive trait that overrides any perceived personal shortcomings. A person who struggles with feelings of inferiority or insecurity may join an association because of it's standing in the community or it's high recognition. Unlike introjection where a person adopts certain behaviors, values, or attitudes, this defense is strictly about begin seen as successful by affiliation.	
Introjection	Introjection can be considered the opposite of projection. Unlike projection where a person may accuse others of an unacceptable impulse that themselves struggle with, introjection is when a person adopts and internalizes values or beliefs of others. Like other defenses this can be compensatory as it relieves the person of responsibility for their own reality of having to evaluate and set their own standards. In other cases, it can relieve feelings of inferiority where characteristics that a person sees as valuable in others is internalized by changed behaviors or appearances themselves. These can be healthy defenses like when a child takes on characteristics of a parent. Maladaptive use of this defense would be a spouse who takes on the values of their racist partner in order to avoid internal tension and manage incongruences.	

Defense	Minimally Effective / Maladaptive (Purpose / Examples)	What I want to do instead …
Projection	The Projection defense serves as a diversion from a person's internal reality of unacceptable impulses by pointing the finger at someone else and blaming them for the same impulse. Whoever that target is, it's basically someone stepping in the line of fire of someone else's internal struggle and paranoia of being *"discovered"*. It may be a kid at school accusing someone wrongly of doing or feeling something that is not true when they themselves are having anxiety provoking feelings.	
Rationalization / Intellectualization	Rationalization is something we all tend to do occasionally. It is often used when someone has a perceived failure or shortcoming and is not able to deal with the problematic feelings of disappointment. It can be an attempt to convince self and/or others that the reason for the "*failure*" was due to uncontrollable circumstances by intellectualizing and using logic. For example, someone who doesn't get the job may dismiss the rejection by pointing at too many over-qualified applicants or that they just had a bad day. It may also be the person who does something wrong and having to apologize causes anxiety, so they try to justify it instead. Essentially, this defense is about maintaining integrity and saving face for a bruised ego.	
Reaction Formation	Reaction Formation is a conscious surfacing and translation of a repressed impulse that is not deemed appropriate by prosocial rules. Rather than try to hide undesirable emotions and internal discord the person does the opposite in attitude or behavior in an attempt to override the reality of their true feelings and perceptions. It's in essence an exaggerated and poignant coverup. In Freudian terms it's believed to only occur with one person or "object" but other discussions have risen around broader cultural contexts. A person who would like to put a coworker in their place may instead make a point to be overly polite and courteous. It can be the son who hates his parents but knows that the "*rules*" say to respect your father and mother, so he goes out of his way to obsessively "*prove*" his respect. It can be the person who has racist views yet marries someone of color.	
Regression	Regression is similar to fixation and is an attempt to return to a place of earlier comfort to avoid difficult situations and feelings. Unlike fixations that required ongoing attention and maintenance to avoid discomfort, regression is less rigid and circumstantially temporary. This can be the adult who pulls the covers over their head and stays in bed all day when there are trials and tribulations instead of dealing with them. It can be the child who has been doing things independently for months yet when the parents separate, the child begins to demand help and attention with everything. With both children and adults, life transitions that destabilize tend to prompt a return to earlier defaults.	

Defense	Minimally Effective / Maladaptive (Purpose / Examples)	What I want to do instead …
Repression	Repression is a process of forcing undesirable impulses not deemed acceptable by a person's environment, society or other "*rules*", into hiding to avoid their reality. It is usually an adaptive coping mechanism that begins around age 5 that teaches the brain to exclude difficult thoughts and emotions from awareness. This defense is a part of the core of all the other mechanisms. Children usually learn "*right from wrong*" by some form of punishment. For example, if a child hits his little brother. The aggressive impulse behind it may not have felt bad but it sure felt bad to get yelled at, spanked or be disapproved of by mom/dad/parent for doing it. Later as an adult, when the person experiences a similar impulse, they may feel a grave sense of anxiety even if they didn't hit someone, the two are paired by conditioning. It can be the same for the kid who is teased or laughed at in class for crying. Whenever that child feels those same impulses whether aggression or other strong emotion later in life, it can create discomfort and anxiety. In order to cope they may develop some automated behavioral habit to distract and cover it up if they don't learn how to process those impulses in a more effective way.	
Sublimation	The Sublimation defense involves diverting sexual/aggressive energy to other channels. This can be adaptive and healthy, like sports, arts, or hobbies to deal with internal anxious impulses. Those activities may then also serve as positive reinforcements if that the person receives accolades for their effort. This is similar to Displacement or Projection but does not involve transferring feelings or accusations on someone else. Unlike the teen without a voice who stuffs food in place of verbal expression, with sublimation that teen may instead start an activist club for other teens against injustices in high school.	

Adapted from Corey, G., 2009; Feist & Feist, 2006.

Any other observations?

_____

_____

_____

_____

_____

_____

_____

_____

_____

_____

_____

_____

_____

The Break-Out Plan

Breaking free from old habits, rules, messaging, and internal negative voices is a process that involves *Differentiation*[18]. In order to break free of old patterns and habits there must be a plan with a target. For example, in the case of differentiation it's becoming aware of when you are operating by default and using go-to's rather than being intentional. In this journal exercise consider what changes you identified in your notes and list the top three.

Habits You Want To Change

1. _____
2. _____
3. _____

Patterns You Want to Change

1. _____
2. _____
3. _____

Defaults That Need to Go

1. _____
2. _____
3. _____

Go-To's To Let Go Of

1. _____
2. _____
3. _____

New Routine

The only time you can intervene with yourself is every day, not tomorrow or yesterday. Spending time in the past or future is always futile when it comes to engagement and personal power. Knowing what you now know about your routine, habits, and patterns, set a plan for catching yourself in those moments of internal compromise or external pressure to think and do something new and eventually impact how you feel. In essence, to recondition yourself by awareness and exposure to new information and healthier perspectives using the psychological phenomena describe in previous weeks. In November and December, you'll be building on these concepts to secure a platform that you can launch the new year from and maybe even find success in those New Year's Resolutions.

What we usually tend to do when trying something new is try something 'entirely' new. However, introducing something new can be tricky if there isn't a good natural fit. Something that can help is to build from what you are already doing right. Here are two areas to consider:

What are you already doing that is working for you, like a good habit or something that keeps you on track and moving forward?

_____

_____

_____

_____

_____

_____

_____

_____

Something that can trip us up is "time". When we think it's taking too long or we compare to others, we can grow wearing of continuing to put in the effort. However, changing neurology to establish a habit can take anywhere from 2 – 6 weeks with consistent effort. Making it automated and easily accessible to execute can take a few months. It all depends on intersections of environmental conditions, stress, beliefs, and motivational variables. If you reflect on the last time that you pushed your limits, how long into those timelines were you successful? What would it take for you to make it all the way for a few months this time? What have you tried so far that worked even a little? How long did it take before the hamster wheel won again? These are the variables you need to consider and push beyond rather than comparing to others.

_____

_____

_____

_____

_____

_____

_____

_____

_____

_____

_____

_____

What does your ideal routine look like and what would you need to keep in mind in terms of those defaults, go-to's, and psychological phenomena to stay on track?

Morning Routine

_____
_____
_____
_____
_____
_____
_____

Daytime Reminders

_____
_____
_____
_____
_____
_____
_____
_____
_____
_____

Evening Routine

_____
_____
_____
_____
_____
_____
_____
_____
_____

If you are struggling with a habit that is impairing your ability to live life in a way that gives you a sense of satisfaction or it's causing problems, it may be time to find a professional counselor or addictionology specialist to navigate the transition off the hamster wheel.

Any other notes you'd like to capture?

November ~ Time

"Time is a currency you can only spend once". - Unknown

November can be a busy month with the holiday season fast approaching. You may be excited or dreading it or be somewhere in between. Up until this time you have spent the year examining your values, needs, boundaries, strengths, habits, relationships, and self-care. In this chapter you'll have opportunity to see what you've incorporated and identify areas that you still want to change or gaps that you want to fill.

The four main tasks for the month include answering the following questions:

1. How are you spending your time? Take Inventory of your time to know what you are investing in.

2. What is your return on investment? Working within your level of trust of time: is there enough, too much, and are you doing what you "*truly*" want to do?

3. How do factors of overestimation, underestimation, procrastination, and to-do lists influence you?

4. How can you make time work for you? Establishing an ideal and reasonable layout for how you spend your time to honor your values, needs, and boundaries.

Here's an initial prompt to get you thinking about "*time*": What do you believe to be the biggest problems for you in managing your time and what would you like to change?

_____
_____
_____
_____
_____
_____
_____
_____

"Anything that costs you your peace, is too expensive."
– Unknown

Week 1 ~ Where'd the Time Go?!

Time gets away from us. What we hope to do and what we actually do may not find an easy match. But all change begins with awareness. If you really want to make the best use of your time and understand where it's going you must first take inventory of how you are spending it.

While our tendency is to look back and make some generalizations about where time went, that casual reflection may be the first point of error because the devil is in the details as the saying goes. Things must be broken down into smaller pieces to find points of management.

This week the focus will be on observing what you do and reflecting daily. Similar to the exercise you did for *Goals* in January, you'll be monitoring yourself regarding activities. However, this time by the hour – yes, hourly self-check-ins.

On the next page you'll find a Time Tracking Table you can use as or make a copy to fold up and keep with you during the day. Here are some tips for using the table and making the most of this exercise:

1. **1 week**. Choose one week from start to finish, 7 days, where you'll take time to reflect.

2. **Top of the hour**. At the turn of the hour take a moment to think about how you spent the majority of the past hour. Be brief in your description by using categorical highlights. For example, *work, school, friends, social media, internet, eating, meeting, nap etc.*

3. **Reminders**. Starting a new process, task, or habit can take a few tries, even a couple of weeks so don't be hard on yourself if you forget to do this the first few days. Use your phone or a calendar reminder to stay on track and hold yourself accountable. If you miss an hour or more, don't worry about it. You can reflect at the end of the day for those times. The hours that you were successful can serve as mile marker reminders of what happened during the ones that you didn't make a note.

4. **Thoughts, feelings, actions**. In your evening reflections consider how the day's activities influenced your actions, thoughts, and feelings.

5. **Observations**. There is an open journal area after the Table to jot down some of your observations once you have completed the inventory. As always take your time and be as honest as you possible to make the most of this journaling exercise.

Time Tracking Table

	Monday	Tuesday	Wednesday	Thursday	Friday	Saturday	Sunday
6am							
7am							
8am							
9am							
10am							
11am							
NOON							
1pm							
2pm							
3pm							
4pm							
5pm							
6pm							
7pm							
8pm							
9pm							
10pm							
11pm							
12-5am							

Time Observations

Was there anything that surprised you about your inventory findings? You can also revisit your findings in January's "*Got Time*" exercise for comparisons. Notice any differences between now and then?

_____

_____

_____

_____

_____

_____

_____

What were you doing then that you aren't doing now or vice versa? And, what would you like to get back to doing that was working for you?

_____

_____

_____

_____

_____

Were there times of high stress, frustration, or self-defeat talk in your mind with any of your daily activities? If so, which ones stood out the most and which ones kept you from doing what you intended to do?

_____

_____

_____

_____

_____

_____

_____

_____

_____

_____

_____

_____

_____

_____

_____

Any other observations or reflections you want to make a note of?

_____
_____
_____
_____
_____
_____
_____
_____
_____
_____
_____
_____
_____
_____
_____
_____
_____
_____
_____
_____
_____
_____
_____
_____
_____
_____
_____
_____
_____
_____
_____
_____
_____
_____
_____

Week 2 ~ The ROIs

The hot topic of finance and Wallstreet is always the "*ROI*" – return on investment. What will you get back based on what you put in and do the benefits outweigh the risks to make it worth your while? Unlike money that can compound based on interest so to get more of it, time is indeed a currency that you can only spend once, and you don't get it back in the same form. No matter how wise you are with your time, you can't get more of it, but the return can be found in other ways.

For example, getting an education. Once you've learned something no one can take that knowledge from you. Similarly, if you invest time in building relationships, taking care of your home or car, even taking care of yourself, those things can mean time well-spent. How? Because you are investing in your support network, having a clean and functional home or car that you can be proud of, not to mention you will feel better the more you invest in taking care of yourself.

The ROIs of time are up to you to define by leveraging that which is most important to you, and that has the potential to bring life satisfaction over time and not only immediate gratification in the moment. For this week, you'll be evaluating your findings from last week's inventory. Here are some prompts to help you think it through.

Time Evaluation

What did you do last week that you didn't want to do – what was necessary and what was unnecessary?

_____
_____
_____
_____
_____
_____
_____
_____

Was there any particular time that you felt was a waste of time with nothing to show for it?

_____
_____
_____
_____
_____
_____
_____
_____

What could you have done differently during that time that is a part of your values and needs or that align with your self-care goals?

_____

_____

_____

_____

_____

What activities did you do because that's *"how you've always done it"*? What was a habit versus intentional?

_____

_____

_____

_____

_____

Was there a to-do list that dictated what you did – did it work for you or keep you from being spontaneous and leverage an unexpected opportunity to meet your needs, tend to what really matters, or practice boundaries?

_____

_____

_____

_____

_____

What did you say "YES" to that you wanted to, could have, or should have said "NO" to?

_____

_____

_____

_____

_____

Which activities were dictated by your perceptions of an ROI, expectations of others or yourself?

_____

_____

_____

_____

_____

If you break down the sequence of steps that occurred both physically and, in your thinking, how did you end up spending the time the way you did? Where was the fork in the road when you could have thought or did something to spend it differently?

_____

_____

_____

_____

_____

_____

_____

_____

_____

_____

_____

_____

What time *was* well-spent and how did you manage it? What steps did you follow in your thoughts or actions to make it happen?

_____

_____

_____

_____

_____

_____

_____

_____

_____

_____

_____

_____

_____

_____

_____

_____

_____

_____

Any other observations you want to capture?

Week 3 ~ Over, Under, and Procrastination

There can be several reasons why we fail to do what we intend to do. When it comes to our time there may be external demands and responsibilities that distract us that we can't control. But then there are the internal demands that only we are in charge of. A common phenomenon that can trip us up include the "to-do-list". We pile on what we want to get done without calculating what it's going to take. We *over-estimate* or *under-estimate* both time and resources. Although, those culprits are beyond processing in this book, this exercise gives you opportunity to take a few days to figure out how you are investing your time and identify if those are playing a role for you.

Time Thieves

The brain needs time to transition between tasks and events. Some people need only a few minutes but during highly demanding tasks the brain and body may require as much as 30 minutes to an hour of transition time. How are you using yours and do you even have it?

Using your week 1 *Time Inventory* reflections identify areas that could be your points of vulnerability. Many things can contribute to draining your proverbial battery and keep you from doing what needs (or you want) to be done at any given moment. Those are the things that tap into your resilience and may be more stressful than others. The only way to combat that is by internal strengths and motivational factors. However, the tendency is to press on regardless. For this journal entry consider the time-spaces you allow yourself. Are you using your strengths to drain your resources, or do you save up for a rainy day in case something else "*comes up*"?

_____
_____
_____
_____
_____
_____
_____
_____
_____
_____
_____

In your inventory, which tasks were more stressful or draining than others?

_____
_____
_____

_____

_____

_____

_____

_____

_____

_____

Consider your values, needs, beliefs etc., what are you investing in and what do you anticipate being the return on your investment? For example, taking a day to do nothing may seem unproductive but it can reenergize you if you are feeling overwhelmed and stressed. A "*waste of time*" is a part of a belief system, be sure you are defining it intentionally and not based on what your "*grandpa*" said or did. Just like your phone needs to have all its apps shut down and reboot once in a while for optimal functioning, your *mind* needs the same. So, what are you doing for relaxation and cutting out the noise? Do you need to connect with people or have your own space? Are your tasks and activities meaningful to you or are they busy-work to meet prosocial and societal "*quotas*"? Keep in mind that scrolling and gaming can stiffen your neck and body just as much as your mind by overstimulation, it can in fact be counterproductive for relaxation. Limit your time or take frequent breaks.

_____

_____

_____

_____

_____

_____

_____

_____

_____

_____

How many hours in the day went to life's basics: safety, sleep, nutrition, physical movement, financial health etc. (consider your notes in the chapter on Self-Care)?

_____

_____

_____

_____

_____

_____

_____

Overestimation

Overestimation doesn't seem like it can be a problem, after all if you give yourself more time than you need, isn't that good? Yes, it can be and if it is working for you then stick with it. However, there are ways it can work against you most of which occur in the planning phase. What does that look like in your world? When you think of things you need to do and write them on your list or look for time-space to get them done, do you ever find yourself thinking *"it's going to take too long"*? Does it sometimes keep you from doing anything or putting it off? Then it is not working for you. Reflect on some ways this may be playing out for you and what you could and want to do to change it.

_____
_____
_____
_____
_____
_____
_____
_____
_____
_____
_____
_____
_____

Underestimation

Underestimation can be discouraging. You set aside time and it's never enough to get things done, right? Although we tend to blame time, the real problem is usually with our own expectations and calculations or lack thereof. The tendency is to set our sights high but then end up low. With more of those situations than successfully finishing projects, that can turn into a false belief that you are simply a person who *"never completes projects"*. But don't be fooled, you may simply need to shift big expectations to reasonable ones that work for you. You could also be stuck in a false positive belief about yourself and your capabilities. You CAN in fact make things work with new awareness and a new strategy.

What things do you find yourself not able to complete or get discouraged about? What were your expectations in attempting those tasks? What was the size of your task in "time" - 30 minutes, 2 hours, 3 days...? Could you have broken it down into smaller pieces to spread them out over other spans of time?

_____
_____
_____

_____

_____

_____

_____

_____

_____

Procrastination

What runs through your mind when you don't want to do something and you find yourself procrastinating? What about when you reflect on something you didn't do, what was it that ultimately kept you from doing it? What process of evaluation did you use with yourself to determine whether you would be successful or not? How did that play into your motivation? Did it have to do with past failed attempts? Was there some inner voice that says, *"it won't work anyway"*? Or, is it *"just going to take too long and be too hard"*? Be honest. Excuses can be internal or externally based. You can in fact keep yourself so busy thinking that you don't do anything. What is it that keeps you stuck and inactive? Task too big, dissenting voices, or truly not enough time?

_____

_____

_____

_____

_____

_____

_____

_____

_____

Any other observations of what tends to steal your time and keep you from doing what you want to do and feel good about? This can be work demands, negative relationships, gaming, scrolling, searching, substance, habits, or addictions?

_____

_____

_____

_____

_____

_____

_____

The To-Do List Phenomenon

To-do lists can be the dark abyss that looms over you or that which keeps you on track. It's up to you to make it work *for* you and not *against* you. If you are someone who relies on or tends to make lists, how is that working for or against you? How often do you look at it? What rules do you have for using it or putting things on it?

_____

_____

_____

_____

_____

_____

_____

_____

_____

_____

To-Do List Rules

Here are some to-do list rule ideas that you can consider when setting up a plan to make time work for you. You can also add your own if you have ones that are already working for you to serve as reminders.

- ☐ Combine all lists into one and keep it in a centrally located and easily accessible place.

- ☐ Instead of a list, use small post it notes and keep them in a central place. Then write only one task on each so you can throw it away vs having a long list staring at you next time.

- ☐ When writing down a task, don't allow a task to consume more than a 90-minute block of time – 15 minutes of prep transition time, 1 hour or less to do it, and 15 minutes of clean-up transition time.

- ☐ Write down the *estimated time* (ET) in minutes next to each task [*clean out car (30m)*]. If you can't write a task in anything less than "*hours*", then it means it must be broken down into smaller actionable items. Do that first then add the ET.

- ☐ Yes, it can be helpful to have a master "*project*" list but that is not the same as "*to-do's*". Keep them separate. One is a larger goal while the other are actions to get you there.

- ☐ Use checkboxes for each task item and check it off once complete – DO NOT allow yourself to put a mark in the box *until* the task is actually *entirely* finished. Some people prefer to draw a line through completed tasks while others find it looks messy. Do what works for you.

☐ Set a time every week, or daily, for a "*to-do list*" check in. The "*thinking*" habit to support that (instead of sitting down and scrolling) can involve a simple question to yourself, "*what can I get done on my list*?". Being able to quickly see how long different tasks will take can help you decide, complete, and feel productive. Find ways to remind yourself which one makes you feel better: scratching something off your list or scrolling?

☐ If you live with a bigger family or others who can do some tasks or part of them, use a delegation strategy. Write them a note asking if they could do "*xyz*" by "*date*". Be sure to be specific about the task, include an ET, tell them why it's important or helpful, ask when they may be able to fit it in, and thank them for considering it. (See sample To-do list on page 21).

What are some other ways that you make to-do lists work for you?

☐ _____

☐ _____

☐ _____

☐ _____

☐ _____

In your inventory, were there specific larger tasks that could be formulated and put into a master Project List?

☐ _____

☐ _____

☐ _____

☐ _____

☐ _____

☐ _____

☐ _____

Week 4 ~ Time Ideals

Within this month's research about yourself, you probably have a pretty good idea about what you want to change, what works, or where the gaps are in terms of investing your time intentionally. Here are some last prompts to help you condense your findings for later reference and as a reminder when time gets away from you.

What's your plan for using a to-do list?

_____

_____

_____

_____

_____

What things will you reintroduce that worked in the past to "*get back to doing*" that were missing from your inventory?

_____

_____

_____

_____

_____

Helping your mind feel settled often involves knowing how, when, and where things fit. What do you need to think/do each day to help your mind calm down when you feel stressed about finishing or getting to a task? For example, one strategy that can work is to remind yourself that "*there's a space/place for that - I'll think about/do something then*". Just make sure that you have set up a workable schedule and are following it consistently. This can be a significant "trust" factor to build confidence and self-esteem with yourself.

_____

_____

_____

_____

_____

How are you reassuring yourself about time? Over, under, or procrastination? What is your plan to catch yourself in the act of doing any of those three and redirect? How can you use your to-do list to help in that?

_____

_____

_____

_____
_____
_____
_____

Which tasks, events, or social encounters are stressful and demands more time-space both in participation and prep/recovery transition? How will you remind yourself about this to accommodate yourself over others demands?

_____
_____
_____
_____
_____

What tasks did you find yourself doing by automation that you want to "*catch yourself*" doing and redirect? What can you fill that space with instead (thoughts or actions)?

_____
_____
_____
_____
_____

What negative habits do you want to find help with or coaching to overcome? What will be your plan for reaching out and to whom?

_____
_____
_____
_____
_____

If your time was "*Fort Knox*" and everything you value was in there, how would you guard it? What are some basic phrases you could use with yourself or others to set time-space boundaries?

_____
_____
_____
_____
_____
_____
_____

What did you do wisely with your time that brought you the biggest return (feeling good and motivated, free or creative, content, productive, or just thinking good thoughts)?

_____

_____

_____

_____

_____

_____

_____

_____

_____

_____

_____

Before you set out to do something, what can you ask yourself in one sentence to make sure it's in your best interest and a good investment of your time? For example, some people like to ask "one week or one year from now, will this matter?"

_____

_____

_____

On the next page there is a table identical to the one you used in your inventory. If you were to design the perfect way to spend your time to gain the most benefit over the course of a week, what would that look like? Use the table to plot that out. You can make a copy of the table if you want to explore different possibilities or simply write with a pencil to make changes as you find the best time-goal for the highest ROI. Before you begin you may want to review and make some notes to remind yourself what is of value to you that must be prioritized. This can include your basic needs identified in chapter 1, relationships, your needs including time-space transitions necessary to reduce stress, your boundaries, or other reflections from your journaling this year.

_____

_____

_____

_____

_____

_____

_____

_____

_____

_____

Time Investment Plan

	Monday	Tuesday	Wednesday	Thursday	Friday	Saturday	Sunday
6am							
7am							
8am							
9am							
10am							
11am							
NOON							
1pm							
2pm							
3pm							
4pm							
5pm							
6pm							
7pm							
8pm							
9pm							
10pm							
11pm							
12-5am							

December ~ Mindfulness

"Don't let your mind travel to where you don't have control. Past, present, or future – choose wisely." ~ Dr. Vic

Mindfulness has become one of those buzzwords that has gotten lost in the shuffle of mental hype. While it tends to be associated with clearing the mind and yoga, there are alternative meanings that do not relate to floating clouds and meditational humming. From a literary standpoint *"mindfulness"* means to be consciously aware of something in the present moment. It's one of the most important words for operationalizing and interpreting the barebone functions of the physiological brain and body. Specifically, the functions of the body's Autonomic Nervous System (ANS).

Think about how easy it is to scroll through social media compared to cleaning the house or having a difficult conversation with your kids or a partner. The brain loves easy stuff that keeps it engaged, even if it keeps you from doing what you should be doing. While we tend explain that as a process of *procrastination* or making *excuses*, as a function, it's simply the brain proposing to the mind the lesser of two evils, the path of least resistance.

If you were to choose the difficult path, the ANS would immediately rise to the occasion. You'd feel some degree of anxiety as a signal that discomfort is on its way, emotionally or otherwise, and thus to get ready for it. That's not easy and the mind will respond by keeping you seated on the couch and scrolling, right? If you do that too much it can become a habit that is easier to engage in by automation and automation is always a danger zone that requires extra vigilance.

Once the brain learns how to avoid something uncomfortable, it trains you to back off rather than build strength to cope or manage. This can involve everything from backing off from *"hard"* tasks, situations, conversations, or people, all of which can prevent you from freedom of movement in life. It can also keep you from following your dreams or doing what is in your best interest. Life becomes fear-based rather than hope- and action-based.

Being mindful of ANS activation and patterns can give the necessary insight you need to make a difference in your own life towards more control within. How? The body and mind are cyclical and live by certain life-rhythms that track and store sensory information. Over time the brain processes thousands of experiences and in essence classifies them on a spectrum of safe or dangerous. In a process of paired associations, the ANS then tracks reactions, thoughts, feelings, and emotions within you. It uses that information to keep you safe by playing a matching game that is constantly asking – is it a threat? Should I back off? What are my options?

Some of us get false positives with the answers due to a history of adversities that are paired in a maladaptive way, "*it will never work anyway, don't bother*" or "*it will be too painful*", most of which run amuck under our radar. All we know is that all of a sudden, we feel "*anxious*" or "*depressed*", physically in the body and mind. So, we react by automation – that which has kept successfully maintained a distance from conflict with someone or something before. It's protective and mindfulness can tap into that process and redirect it.

Think of it this way, what if you had to intentionally sift through every experience you've ever had to determine what to do, think, or feel moment by moment based on what you are currently faced with? It would be impossible! The human mind doesn't have that kind of processing and retrieval power by explicit command. This is part of the reason why it's easier to give in to an established habit than fight with it. The brain filters the information stored in your brain for you and relies on ANS signals that are paired with those emotions and events.

This is not to say that you are a puppet on a string, the good news is that it can be changed by new and different information over time. Outside of pathology, similar to the way that the original input organized information to make it easier for you to feel anxious or depressed, you can do a *remodel* to create new associations by being mindful. By using mindfulness, you can understand your operations and make predictions based on facts rather than be reactive based on emotional upset.

Lastly, mindfulness can help you avoid exhaustion. The mind has an amazing creative ability to overthink, be curious, imagine, ask the big and tough unanswerable questions, ponder big philosophies, or come up with scenarios that have no basis in reality. However, like going to a lecture, learning a new skill at work, or sitting in class, at the end of the day you may feel drained more than if you were out hiking in the woods. Learning and changing neurological matter in the brain uses electrical impulses above and beyond what is needed for basic day-to-day automated thinking and doing. It doesn't matter if it's positive content or negative. Developing new connections can be like digging a ditch with a spoon, it takes more effort than taking a stroll down memory lane. Mindfulness can center you in the present to avoid going too far into the future or the past. The journaling tasks this month will include:

1. Taking inventory of when your brain, body, and mind may not be in sync.

2. Understanding your thresholds and indicators.

3. Identify tools and techniques that may bring you back into full power.

4. Design sustainable interventions – what's your process and formula?

Remember to paperclip important pages of your discovery journey for easy reference later.

Week 1 ~ Inventory

One of the ways we complicate natural brain-mind-body functions is by going too far into the future or too far into the past in the mind. Why? Neither of those places are within reach of the body or brain and it can be confusing because the overall system has no control there. While the mind is delivering up all sorts of possibilities from memory by spinning on bad recollections or imagining possible catastrophes in the future, the brain-body is trying to execute emotional and psychological safety. However, there is nothing it can do because the actual situation in the mind may not match the options in the present. It can't direct the body to attack or run and hide or play dead so it can feel stuck.

Mindfulness can bring body and brain into the present time-space where the mind then does have control. The trick is to catch yourself when the mind and brain are in different places and bring them into where the body is. For example, spending time online where your mind can travel anywhere, and your brain can get exposure to information that you may not even be consciously aware of, can trip you up. As the brain tries to mitigate and intervene to maintain congruence between mind-body-brain, the conflict can be significant. You may not even know it until you feel off, anxious, angry, even apprehensive, or depressed. While you may not be able to pin-point the issue at the time, one possibility is that your physical and psychological systems are not in sync. Your mind may "*feel*" like something's wrong but when your brain-body look around there's nothing going on. It can make you feel like you're going crazy.

Beyond online influences there are of course other things that can throw you off. If your friend has a problem, maybe you feel their pain. When the boss is a jerk, or the car needs repairs, or family and life's responsibilities and demands exceed your internal wherewithal. Even great and positive things can take you off course. So, what does that look like for you? Maybe you have some things that you identified as stressors in February.

This week you'll be observing yourself to see where your "*system*" is at and the impacts on your state of mind, mood, and activities. Mindfulness is a process that brings awareness to understand your own mind-body-brain congruence. You will use the same process as you have in other chapters. Take a moment at the end of each day to reflect and write down your observations by the chronological <u>facts</u> of the day. Focus on five points for reflection:

1. Events (what you did, what happened, what someone else did)
2. Thoughts (mind and attitude)
3. Emotions (feelings and mood)
4. Physical (what and where did you feel something in your body)
5. Sensory input (sight, sound, touch, smell, and taste – like what did you eat, what were you wearing, was it comfortable, what was the weather like hot/cold etc.).

Day 1

_____
_____
_____
_____
_____
_____
_____
_____
_____
_____
_____
_____

Day 2

_____
_____
_____
_____
_____
_____
_____
_____
_____
_____
_____
_____
_____
_____
_____
_____

Day 3

_____
_____
_____
_____
_____
_____

_____
_____
_____
_____
_____
_____
_____
_____
_____

Day 4

_____
_____
_____
_____
_____
_____
_____
_____
_____
_____
_____
_____
_____

Day 5

_____
_____
_____
_____
_____
_____
_____
_____
_____
_____
_____

_____

_____

_____

Day 6

_____

_____

_____

_____

_____

_____

_____

_____

_____

_____

_____

_____

_____

_____

Day 7

_____

_____

_____

_____

_____

_____

_____

_____

_____

_____

_____

_____

_____

_____

_____

Week 2 ~ A Fork in The Road

Last week you monitored and observed the chronological and factual events such as internal/external physical experiences and psychological states for seven days. You may have identified times when your body, brain, and mind weren't necessarily playing nice with each other. One may have been trying to do something about tomorrow, the other filtering through the past, while the body was trying to do something in the present moment. This week you'll be considering the intersection of events and *when* things may have shifted to change your mood or attitude for the day from either better to worse or the reverse.

In reviewing your notes from last week, take some time to revisit your experiences and identify ones that stood out to you or that had the biggest impact. Instead of looking just at what happened, retrace the timing of events to identify WHEN a change occurred. What was it that led up to it? For example, maybe you had a hard time getting out of bed some days and ran late or everything was fine all week until a certain day. If you were to redesign that day or event, when could you have created a fork in the road to choose a different direction?

Here are some prompts to think through the intersections of how you felt (mood), what you thought (attitude), and your actions on those days and events.

What activities seemed to get you off course and when did they occur?

_____

_____

_____

_____

_____

What was your mind thinking about at the time? What was your body doing? Were mind/body in the same place and tending to the same activity?

_____

_____

_____

_____

_____

How often did you find yourself thinking about the past or future? What was the impact? What did it remind you of?

_____

_____

_____

_____

_____

If you had a <u>difficult day</u> what was the cause-and-effect process?

_____

_____

_____

_____

_____

If you had a <u>good day</u> what was the cause-and-effect process?

_____

_____

_____

_____

_____

Was there something that made you feel connected and grounded to stay focused?

_____

_____

_____

_____

_____

How did you start the day?

_____

_____

_____

_____

_____

How did you end the day, the night before?

_____

_____

_____

_____

_____

When did you feel most in control?

_____

_____

_____

_____

Week 3 ~ What Are You Doing?

In week 1 and 2, you observed and identified the "*what* and *when*" targets of impact, this week you'll be testing out some techniques to see where your controls are. The big questions include: can you actually catch yourself in those "*fork in the road*" moments to change the trajectory of events? Is your "*system*" aligned with your values, needs, and self-care goals in those moments? Are you congruent with time and space in your mind-body-mind system? Who (or what) is in charge of *YOU*?

On the next few pages, you'll find a series of tools that can create "*mindfulness*" in everyday tasks and events. Review the tools and consider which ones you may be able to use to address the areas that you wanted to change. Be as specific as possible, for example, your targets can be thoughts, actions, or feelings, or shifting your appraisal of environmental changes that are out of your control. How did you make sense of them? What do you need to stay focused on? What can you do?

It's easy to go someplace nicer in your mind or check-in on social media instead of deal with tough stuff, but those instances are probably not moving you towards your goals and do not involve your values or needs. They also may be keeping you hostage in life. This is particularly true if you have some habits and patterns of thinking and doing that aren't serving you well. For example, if you had a difficult day last week and you started the day in a compromised state, like running late, that is an opportunity to be mindful rather than passively adopting what your brain usually delivers up which can include: "*well, this day is shot*" or "*the boss is going to be so mad*", "*why can't I get things right*?!". Focusing on what happened, even as recent as the same morning, will keep you in the past where you have no control. It's an opportunity to redirect and focus on what you CAN do. The more you focus on what you didn't do right the less likely you are to plan on trying something new tomorrow to change it.

You can decide now what not to allow the mind to be distracted and guilty about. In that case you'll want to catch yourself heading down that pathway by taking responsibility and being determined by formulating a plan to avoid the same issue in the future. If you don't change that internal process, the second you park at making excuses or trying to avoid a hard reality, the brain stops looking for solutions and it goes where it's more comfortable.

Another common situation is if you tend to hit moments of idleness or feeling overwhelmed during the day. That can be a split in the system and a perfect opportunity to back off, do a check-in, and get your system into the same time-space. There is one main rule for moment-by-moment congruence is that it must involve all three facets of your system: brain, mind, and body. For this week choose from no more than one or two tools per day and decide to keep them at the forefront of your mind and at which points you'll use them.

Tools

There are a wealth of "*mindfulness*" tools and techniques available today. Do a Google search and you'll end up with millions of results and as with any resource, not all of them work for everyone all of the time. Finding what works for you can involve trial and error. But whether you've tried them before or not, or even believe in mindfulness, there is an unavoidable physical reality of how your mind, brain, and body function. Below is some information to help you think it through. If you already have techniques or tools you're using or that friends have recommended, list them here for easy reference or to use over the course of this week.

_____
_____
_____
_____
_____

Metacognition and Indicators

Metacognition[19] is a psychological term that means to be aware of one's own "*thinking*" processes. You can use this as a tool of knowledge by training yourself to do check-ins throughout the day or at specific points (see the "*Target*" section later in this chapter) such as when you feel most vulnerable in the afternoon when the day has dragged on, or in the morning if you woke up feeling "*off*". The key question is: **"*what am I thinking*?"**. Try it out for a day by asking yourself this question as often as you can and make a note in the sections below. You may want to revisit your journaling notes related to vulnerabilities in chapters on Stressors, Relationships, Boundaries, and Time for other ideas of what to target.

☐ Stressors

_____
_____

☐ Relationships

_____
_____

☐ Boundaries

_____
_____

☐ Time

_____

According to research[20], our experiences need to have a match with our perceptions and world-views and when they don't, we subconsciously adjust our interpretation to make things fit. For example, if a friend sets you up on a date and says, *"you'll really like him, he's great!"*, then during the date you may look for things that are *"great"*. However, If you don't find signs that align with what your friend said or what you define as *"great"* then there can be an incongruence. You may question what to trust more; your friend or your definition of *"great"*. Either way you'll adjust according to what you decide. You will make it about your friend, yourself, or the guy *"he's not that great"*. However, if you aren't aware of those cognitive processes behind how you feel and how you are making sense of things, you may run for the hills or stay longer than you'd like with the guy.

Using metacognition as a mindfulness tool can make it a conscious decision and not one based on habitual patterns of *thinking, feeling,* or *doing* like always blaming yourself or others but looking at things objectively and challenging them. Knowing your indicators of incongruence can help you decide when and what to question. Take a moment to list some of your findings that may have been points of congruence or incongruence in the past week that you also want to recognize in the future to apply metacognitive reflection – you can call them internal *"red flags"*. Here are some prompts to get you started.

CONGRUENCE

Congruence[21] is a state of *"being"* where what you believe, value, think, do, and feel all agree. For example, if you believe that you are a productive member of society and that such a person recycles, then regardless of how much work it is, you may do it anyway and as a result you feel good. It can also be in terms of *Mood-Memory Congruence* or what I refer to as the *"lollipop effect"*. When you feel sad it is easier to recall and think about sad things more than happy things. Just watch a toddler in the checkout lane when denied a piece of candy – suddenly, they begin a diatribe of recollections covering everything bad that has ever happened only to conclude with statements that *"nothing is fair"* and they *"never get anything I want!"*.

The brain looks for a fit to make sure all aspects of your being align. The brain likes that *matchy-matchy* process and will adjust to maintain it, sometimes at all costs. If you are sad and encounter someone who is happy you may feel even worse and thus try to adjust by bringing them to your realm of mood or avoid them altogether. You may also try to justify and convince them of why being sad is necessary for you rather than let them create a sense of incongruence by making you happy.

I feel most grounded when I _____

_____

I think most clearly in the / when I _____ (morning, evening, alone, quiet/noise etc.)

_____

When I see / talk to _____ I feel connected, a part of a community _____

_____

Something that keeps me focused on what's important is _____

_____

When I _____ it helps me stay calm

_____

An activity that makes me feel productive, valuable, or engaged is _____

_____

Because of who I am, and how I see myself, I must _____

_____

My friends think I'm _____ so I _____

_____

My family thinks I'm _____ so I _____

_____

A "good" person is someone who (you may want to revisit your response to this on page 99)

_____

_____

INCONGRUENCE

By contrast to congruence, like the case where a sad person sees a happy person, incongruence means there is a mismatch by values, beliefs, mood, or the perceptions of what is appropriate as in schemas or scripts in different contexts – what you are feeling, thinking, and doing versus how you think it should be. The most devastating of congruence effects relates to "illness identity"[22]. This is a part of a process of internalization and integrated regulation. A physical example of how that works is that if the room is too hot you are more likely to go and adjust the heat settings than if you feel ok or are comfortable, aka have "congruence". Illness Identity is the same type of comfort adjustment that creates "fit" which is a logic of "if A is true then B must follow". It is a close cousin to Self-Fulfilling Prophecy[23] effects. If you believe that someone doesn't like you, you are less likely to be open and share yourself with them which may be interpreted by them as a sign that you are not interested in being friends. In turn, they back off and what you believe is essentially confirmed and becomes the true reality.

With psychiatric diagnoses this is a particularly significant danger-zone because what you think and feel matter. Just like your immune system will be affected by a virus, the introduction of a false positive or suggested possibility influences what you look for and how you respond. There is no pill that can fix that. If you have been diagnosed with a mental disorder your brain is more likely to seek out a match in behavior, mood, and environment to that schema and narrative. It's one of the influencers of *help-seeking* versus *help-avoidance* behaviors[24].

Some people believe mental illness is a terminal state without resolve or a permanent tag on one's reputation while others use it to then find a fit in life. They seek out groups or chats that are of similar mindset and struggle. Unfortunately, this can create a mood-memory congruence effect that sustains a condition rather than helps pull them out of it. In that way, incongruence can be as harmful as congruence. The best approach is to understand how both operate for you and choose which direction you want to go. Sometimes finding professional help with a psychologist or counselor who specializes in this area can be a game changer to break free of established mind-patterns.

Reflect on the past week and see where you may have been in a state of incongruence. Maybe it was in conversation where you felt a need to convince someone of something or a situation just didn't *"feel"* right. What did you think was going on? How did you respond? What "adjustments" did you find yourself making in thinking, feeling, doing, or perceptions to make things fit?

Critical Thinking

So, what can you do in times when things don't align or aren't necessarily a problem to make sure you're staying on track? One way is to differentiate between times of passive thinking and active thinking. One uses an intentional appraisal process while the other simply does what it's *"told"*. By the way, it's always easier to just play along with the brain's automated stuff when you are stressed and under pressure. That should be one of your consistently noted markers in any day and event. The second you find your mind and brain headed towards the pit of doom and gloom it's always time to take action rather than passively follow along. Critical thinking can be one of those knowledge tools that you can use to question whether you should go along or try something else. Here are some questions to use in your decision-making tree of whether to entertain an idea, thought, and feeling or move on to finding something more useful and productive to work towards your goals, meeting your values and needs, and having congruence.

- ○ Why am I doing this?
- ○ What information may I be missing?
- ○ What am I taking for granted?
- ○ What are the implications of my thoughts?
- ○ What assumptions am I making?
- ○ Are there other points of view or ways to reason this out?
- ○ What expectations do I have?
- ○ What do I need more clarification about?
- ○ Why does this matter?
- ○ What would my _____ say about this?
- ○ Is what I'm thinking relevant to the situation?
- ○ What conclusions am I drawing and based on what facts?
- ○ What problem am I trying to solve?
- ○ Who holds the problem?
- ○ Whose responsibility is it?
- ○ What can I do about it, really?
- ○ What can I do differently?
- ○ Do I need to step away to collect myself, sleep on it, consult with someone?

If any of these resonated with you perhaps you also remembered some of your own questions that have helped you stop and think or take a different more "*sensible*" course of action before. Make a note of those as well in order to design some ways you can intervene with yourself to question it or use grounding techniques to catch your breath. Remember sometimes the best question with self and others is to ask for more time before acting, speaking, or settling on anything. When in doubt contact a neutral person with no personal agenda or bias in order to process it through.

_____

_____

_____

_____

_____

_____

Breathing Matters

In other segments we discuss breathing as a mindfulness activity. It is probably one of *the* most important aspects of managing your internal states whether physical or psychological. Your body's circulatory system and oxygen are key for the mind to access important information stored in your brain. Without those basic operations carbon dioxide and other wasters would not be removed nor would nutrients be delivered. This means that cognitive neurological pathways that are normally accessible may become blocked off while the body focuses on restoring physical order. Remember, the brain and mind use electrical impulses to function which means energy is used up. In the event of an "outage", conservation becomes key, like not opening the fridge constantly, the body redirects and the mind suffers. Like when stress hits and you get sent into an instant funk, like an inability to think straight, racing pulse, or some sense of panic. For more on that you can revisit the chapter on Stressors.

Although you can't directly control your blood flow or pressure, you can use your breath to do so indirectly. How? By breathing intentionally. This is like an override in case of an emergency where you are forcing the pressure of flow rather than waiting for services to run their course. You can exercise to increase energy, whether jumping jacks, a walk, dancing, singing loudly, screaming, and taking long deep breaths and holding the breath in between and then letting that out slowly. Closing your eyes while you are doing this and centering on that internal activity and restoration can shut out the external noise and have an even greater and immediate impact. It may take practice but once your mind, body, and brain know where to meet during a fire drill it will become easier and more accessible than the panic event. It can start by something as simple as knowing when you are approaching a funk and asking yourself am I breathing? Then apply a technique that will work for you.

For this exercise, search the internet for video resources, Instagram posts, or websites that provide breathing exercises for stress reduction, diaphragmatic breathing techniques, or similar mindfulness tools. Try some on for size to see which ones may be easiest for you to remember and use. To start, spend time over a period of a few days to catch yourself in moments when you are "*holding*" your breath. When you do, find a place to retreat to for a few minutes (a closet, your car, or bathroom) or try it where you are, close your eyes and focus on breathing.

How did that feel? Did it give you a sense of momentary relief? Which place did you try it in? What would you need to change to make this work for you? The more you practice this the easier it will be for your mind and body to adopt it as a matter of habit to maintain control internally.

___

_____

_____

_____

_____

_____

_____

_____

_____

_____

_____

_____

_____

What's Your "411"?

Grounding is probably my personal favorite to get to the bottom of options for being in the moment and not letting the noise get the best of me. You can frame it anyway you'd like but it's essentially calling in your truth of what is relevant in any given space of time.

I'm sure you've had days when emotions and stressful situations impair whatever calm you did have when you left the house in the morning. Good or bad it can send you high on energy towards fixing something or planning for the future and quickly escalate to a 30,000ft mission! Grounding brings you back down to recharge and stop the noise whether internal or otherwise. It is an intentional activity that draws your attention to the reality of a present experience like paying attention to how your breath feels going in through your nose, your lungs, and ultimately exhaling, or doing a mental scan of your body. It requires all your mental faculties, senses, and physical participation. Picture the bullet scene in the movie *The Matrix* where everything is either still or moving in slow motion. It allows the characters to pause and take a look around to collect themselves, mindfulness can do that in your mind. The key is to find what works for you.

How can you do that? Below is a list of commonly cited mindfulness activities. For some people it is important to find a space that is void of activity. However, with trial and error as well as practice you can find ways to be mindful during almost any situation. How long you'll need to "*do it*" depends on the chronic state, type of, and frequency of "*interference*" (stress for example) that you have been experiencing. Remember it can take anywhere from minutes to a full hour to calm the ANS after a real or perceived "*threat*" is removed. Mindfulness activities used on a regular basis can train your ANS to catch situations early enough where your internal state does not escalate to extreme heights.

Did it work? The best gauge of what you need to make this work will always be your own sense of calm which is why it's important to do a check in with yourself after trying one of the strategies for a while to see how you feel – body, mind, and brain power. Are you thinking a little clearer? Do you feel a bit more removed from the pressure? Are you less inclined to engage and fuel emotional upset – others and your own? Has the tension in your shoulders, neck, gut, head, or other physical areas lessened? Since the ANS touches on every part of your internal system including digestion and blood pressure, you may even feel a relief if you struggle with tension or other headaches or stomach problems. You may want to consult with your doctor about the option of using a combined medical and mindfulness intervention approach if your struggle is severe.

What if it doesn't work? Some strategies may work better in some situations but not others, time, place, and practice to get to a routine of use, may be necessary to consider. For example, trying to do creative art during lunch when you have a stack of work or pressing meetings to get back to may put more pressure on you rather than relieve it. Sometimes the answer is simply a 30-minute walk or even 20-minute nap to give a boost to the adrenals. When doing any mindfulness activity, you may want to start by shutting out distractions like technologies (phone, TV, Radio, tablet etc.) where someone could speak to you, a notification can pop up, or some other noise can enter into your fields of sensory perception beyond the mindful activity.

- ☐ Doodling or drawing
- ☐ Creating art, like sculping or painting
- ☐ Playing an instrument or singing
- ☐ Closing your eyes, listening to calming or instrumental music and the various instruments
- ☐ Imagery and visualization of someplace peaceful
- ☐ Walking barefoot and making a mental note of how it feels on your feet
- ☐ Listening to nature sounds
- ☐ Look out the window and watch the trees sway in the breeze
- ☐ Go to a river and watch the water flow over the rocks or ocean side to watch the waves
- ☐ Guided or other types of meditation
- ☐ Mindful eating – how does the food taste, feel, smell
- ☐ Mindful listening – reflecting on what is said versus thinking of what to say
- ☐ Caring for plants or gardening
- ☐ Doing a physical puzzle (word, visual or other kind)
- ☐ Getting lost in a good (physical) book

Here's a set of cognitive questioning you can use to challenge busy thoughts and ground yourself in the moment. If there is a stressful point to the day, find a place to retreat for a few minutes. Mute the phone, hold all calls, turn off your monitor, close the door to your office, put up the "back in 5-minutes" sign, go out to your car, or simply lean back in your chair and stop doing what you are doing. While breathing normally, answer these with as much descriptive detail as you can:

- What do you see?
- What can you touch?
- What is that like? Describe it.
- What do you smell?
- What do you feel in your body?
- What is the temperature in the room or place you are in?
- What do you hear?
- How does your body feel where you are standing or sitting? Describe it.
- Who / what is in the room?
- What colors do you see?
- What shapes do you see?
- What types of thoughts are floating through your mind?

The bottom line is simply to bring your mind, brain, and body into alignment with the present situation for congruence. As you can see, the way to do that comes in many shapes and sizes but always involves reducing emotional engagement by factual observations about the sensory and physical self within the current environment. Over the course of a few days or a week, give some of these.

Which ones did you try that resonated with you? When and how did you apply them? Did you personalize the strategy by adding a question or changing the type of activity to make it work?

_____

_____

_____

_____

_____

_____

_____

_____

_____

_____

Catch & Release

The wonderful world of acronyms does have a positive side, they can provide quick access to information in the brain that otherwise would remain hidden without some explicit cue ("*trigger*"). By using an acronym, you can create a sort of "*bookmark*" in the brain that is paired with an experience, action, thought, or feeling of relief. For example, If you want to lose weight and find it difficult to remember how to fight through the cravings, or if you are trying to be more mindful and want to remember to try out a technique, one word can be that reminder. Put it on a sticky-note or in a calendar task that pops up throughout the day on your phone to cue up certain information that will be useful in the moment.

For example, using the mnemonic *S.T.O.P.* whenever you feel "panic" coming on you can redirect to using mindfulness techniques or H.A.L.T. to be mindful that when things feel off or desperate there may be a reasonable explanation. Remember that one word is much easier than trying to remember a dozen words to stop what you are doing, close your eyes for a moment and look inward, take a deep breath, or to observe your surroundings and how you are feeling to then proceed to doing only what needs the moment and W.I.N.! If you're old-school you can trim that even further by saying *"stop and smell the roses"*. The key is to find what works for you to intervene and redirect to be mindful and not have a split-action-event between brain, mind, and body. Catch and inhale the good and then release the bad. Here are some additional mnemonics and brief-tools that I often recommend and use.

5/7 Rule[25] – the mind can juggle 5-7 things at a time by basic function of recall and processing. The rule is that if you hit 7, your system is maxed-out but even after 3 or 4 you may begin to feel compromised. What is your range in order of importance and where is your cut off? Here is a basic chart to use when considering your daily 5/7 rules:

Normal range of resilience:

1. Must do _____
2. Want to do/self _____
3. Need to do/others _____
4. Can do for self/others _____

Danger zones:

5. Unexpected daily/life stressors _____
6. Yellow light: if I hit the gas and ignore this _____ it could cause _____
7. Red light: if I run through this _____ a crash is imminent.

75/25 Rule[26] – nothing is perfect. Give yourself 25% space and time to breathe and make mistakes, and 75% of the time to do it *"right"*. Then afford the same to others. You can change the percentages to whatever works for you in accordance with your Self-Care plan. When you feel like you're not doing anything right and nothing is working, remind yourself that it doesn't have to be perfect. Dust yourself off and focus on moving forward.

ALEC[27] – This acronym is designed to be used as a four-step process to strike up a conversation with someone who seems disconnected, distanced, or socially isolating. But it can work for you too. When you find yourself or others in a pit of darkness question it and be supportive by asking, listening, encouraging, and following up:

A – Ask: R U Ok? Be friendly, relaxed or supplement with *"how are you doing*?" or *"what's been happening*?". Sometimes people aren't ready to talk so don't push. This tool is to open the door and provide a place the person can come to.

— L – Listen without judgment. Don't rush the conversation or interrupt.

— E - Encourage action. What have you done before when this happens? How can I support you? What's something you can do this week or even today?

— C - Check-in. Let someone know they've been on your mind and you're wondering how things have been going.

ALGEE[28] – Similar to ALEC, this is another mnemonic that can be used either with self or others. As hard as it may be to step up for yourself, it can be equally hard to know what to do for others and we can feel bad that we didn't or aren't sure how to help. In the case of being faced with someone else's distress here is a process to use and encourage seek help:

— Assess risk of harm

— Listen nonjudgmentally

— Give reassurance and information

— Encourage person to get professional help

— Encourage other supports to self-help, strategies

ABC's of REBT[29] – This Rational Emotive Behavior Therapy technique can help regain some ground by tapping into the logic of events in relationship to difficult feelings. When feeling stressed or compromised it's easy to focus on emotions rather than facts. Here are the versions of this to teach yourself to be mindful that just because something feels really bad, that doesn't mean it is or that something is wrong. Everything has a reason and sometimes you won't know it until later. All you need to do is get through this moment and the few that may come after to wait for the answers and solutions to come to you. To create more relevance around these you can also look for your own examples in relevant chapters like Beliefs, Stressors, and Boundaries.

A. Activating event or situation that triggers reaction/response. Skills: manage activating event. problem solving, assertiveness, social skills, decision-making skills, conflict resolution skills.

B. Beliefs or thoughts that arise in you. Skills: change beliefs and thoughts by reframe, avoid rationalization and maladaptive coping patterns, use guided imagery/visualization, use humor or irony, use adaptation to expose and extinct fear beliefs, dispute thoughts with critical thinking.

C. Consequences like distressing emotions and difficult feelings. Skills: to face and manage consequences using relaxation, hypnosis, meditation, breathing or other meditative technique that is present-moment-focused or future-focused – nothing is permanent, this is temporary.

F.O.C.U.S.[30] – If you've ever experienced discomfort or unease in social situations, this can serve as a tool to get grounded in a focus that is outside of your own insecurities by using mindful communication. When you are faced with a person that intimidates you or that you want to be more mindful with, like a partner or close friend, here is a different focus that you can practice anywhere and anytime to build up a new strength:

Feel - feet on floor and your back against your chair.
Observe - listen, see the person. Pay attention to visual facts, take mental note but do not judge.
Curious - be curious: why, how, when, where, needs, values, boundaries?
Understand - the other person: why, ask how you can help or what they need.
Stop - before you respond, reflect. What are they really saying? Not sure? Be curious to understand, ask for clarity or more information *"tell me more"*, *"what is that like for you?"*...

H.A.L.T.[31] – This task is simple, what is your upset feelings, thoughts, and inclinations telling you? What does your mind-body-brain-need? Meet your needs at your baseline first. Are you:

- ☐ Hungry?
- ☐ Angry?
- ☐ Lonely?
- ☐ Tired?

Opt-Out[32] – The Opt-Out strategy is about minding others emotional, cognitive, and physical space as well as your own. Asking for space or time to think before responding and giving an *"out"* for a person you're with if the topic or question you are presenting them with is not something they've had a chance to think about: *"can I get back to you on that?"*, *"can you give me some time to think about that?"*, *"would you mind if we talked about _____?"*.

RESPECT-FUL[33] – Being mindful involves much more than being kind and present in our own world but also how we intersect with other's worlds. Relationships can intimidate and confuse us and being respectful can create safety for you and others. While the RESPECTFUL model is designed for counselors to use in their work with clients, it can also serve as a valuable reminder of how we can all be kind in our mind. I have adapted the wording to incorporate personal responsibility while retaining the supportive message of being sensitive to diversity and multiculturalism. As the saying goes *"everyone is struggling with something, be kind"*.

R – Respect, Response, Religion, Race, Responsibility. Taking responsibility for your response, not everyone believes the same be mindful of your assumptions and jokes.

E – Encourage - no excuses for negative behaviors

S – Safety, Sexuality, Sensitivity, Space. mind personal space and self-control

P – Psychological Development, Patience – be patient and polite

E – Ethnicity, Engagement, Economic status - exercise equity and empathy

C- Cultural orientation, Considerate, Cooperate, Collaborate - be considerate and cooperative

T – Trust, Trauma - and believe the best"

F – Family history

U – Unique Characteristics/physical

L – Language, Location

S.T.O.P. – Whenever you feel "panic" coming on you can redirect to using mindfulness techniques. Remember that one word is much easier than trying to remember a dozen word – stop what you are doing, take a deep breath and close your eyes, observe your surroundings and how you are feeling, proceed to doing only what needs the moment and task requires by focusing on that.

W.I.N.[34] – *What's Important Now?* We all want a "*win*" don't we? A day without having to tackle something or fight with ourselves. One way to stay focused and win is to pull yourself back to the present task at hand and do what you can. Whenever you feel like the day is getting away from you either in your mind or physical reality, pause and give yourself a W.I.N. by only doing what absolutely must be done that day or hour.

Power Tools and Strengths

In the previous chapter on Strengths, you identified several "*power tools*". Some of them may have included reminders of your prior accomplishments or power words and phrases that resonate with you. These can be important fillers useful for replacing negative talk that you engage in with yourself. It's a part of positive psychological principles as well as cognitive behavioral approaches where you choose to focus on the positive and redirect or reframe the negative. Other tools of strength can be recognizing when you are making progress. For example, you identified specific targets in your Self-Care. Begin to look for those improvement measures that you set for yourself rather than focusing on what you didn't accomplish – as in allowing your mind, brain, and body to go in different directions. You can only be successful moment by moment and every big success had many mini-steps thereof. Take some time to reflect on those chapters and remind yourself of what the most useful tools were. Could they work for you now to be more mindful throughout your day or give you a different point of focus?

Power Words

_____
_____
_____
_____
_____
_____
_____

Power Phrases or Sayings

_____
_____
_____
_____
_____
_____

Good Memories and/or Successes

_____
_____
_____
_____
_____
_____
_____

Are there other tools, techniques, or resources that you find useful in managing what you are doing?

_____
_____
_____
_____
_____
_____
_____
_____
_____
_____

"Sometimes your joy is the source of your smile, but sometimes your smile can be the source of your joy."
– Thich Nhat Hanh

Week 4 ~ Target Process & Rules

While it would be impossible to list all the things you may want to target using mindfulness, there are specific controls that only exist in three specific spaces of time each day, that's your *time-space*. That space runs between morning, daytime, and evening and is where you must navigate the past, present, and future.

Think of it like a domino effect. In the evening you can set the tone for your sleep and therefore how and what you wake up to. In the morning you can set the tone for the day. Like a football player scoping out a play and what to tackle to score a goal, you can do the same. Set your focus and keep that focus. Getting to bed on time, reflecting in a healthy way on what did work during the day, making some notes of what you don't want to forget and put things in your calendar. You can prep your time-space for things that are important so that your mind isn't churning on when and how and what – in other words, make it as easy as possible for your mind to do what is most beneficial for you in the long run and to survive the present.

For this journal exercise consider what you are doing during these segments of time and think of what you can do differently as well as what tool or technique you could set aside time to use to stay on track. The goal is to keep synchronicity between what your mind is on, how your brain may be scanning for "*threat*" and possibly alarming you unnecessarily, while doing what you need to do using your physical-self in the moment.

Morning

You've already discovered some aspects of what you do in previous reflections like your routine inventory in Habits and Patters. This week try to be more mindful and target-focused by observing your morning routine by cause-and-effect. What is in your control and what is out of your control? What is your mind on while your body is trying to get ready? How many distractions are you voluntarily letting into your first minutes after opening your eyes? Is your brain able to focus on normal activity like breathing and digestion, or is the stress kicking in before your feet hit the floor?

Mind

_____

_____

_____

_____

_____

Body

_____

_____
_____
_____
_____

Brain

_____
_____
_____
_____
_____
_____

Daytime

At which points of the day do you feel most compromised? What are your mind, body, and brain doing in those experiences in response to it? Are they in agreement or running in different directions trying to make things work? What mindfulness tools might you use to re-center and ground yourself?

Mind

_____
_____
_____
_____
_____

Body

_____
_____
_____
_____
_____

Brain

_____
_____
_____
_____
_____

Evening

The evening may leave you feeling drained or wound up from the day. Bringing closure can be easier said than done. However, it's imperative that you find a way to do that. A full night sleep and rest allows the body, brain, and mind to gather up the day's information and put things into memory storage appropriately. It also gives the body a break and recharges those adrenals which is why the morning is often the best time to set yourself up for success.

The evening is where you can assess whether you're *"burning the candle at both ends"*. If you aren't ending the day on a good note believing that *"you did the best you could and all you could do for today is done"*, it will be harder to start on a good note. It's a vicious cycle to get caught up in and while breaking it can be a bit of work, if you don't, then your health and mind can suffer unfavorable consequences. Even though you may succeed in keeping your mind awake and alert, your body can tell time. The circadian rhythm recognizes when the day is drawing to a close by darkness and other factors. It begins to shut down daytime operations probably well before you do which includes digestion and metabolic processes as well as hormones needed for sleeping. Not honoring those natural processes can be a fight that makes your body retain weight, causes the brain to have cravings, and your mind to act up emotionally.

So, what kind of rest do you get at night? What do you need to feel good when you wake up? Do you wake up rested and energized or dragging yourself out of bed after hitting snooze a dozen times? What is your current routine in the evening? Do you have any special bedtime habits? What are your sleep hygiene practices? When do you allow your mind to shut down from lights, media input, or social engagement? Be honest in your reflections and observations.

Mind

_____
_____
_____
_____
_____

Body

_____
_____
_____
_____
_____

Brain

_____

_____

_____

_____

_____

Your Change Process

Identifying your change process involves paying attention to how long it takes between the time you have an idea of what you want to do and making it happen. The brain needs placeholders before it can make the necessary connections between thoughts and mobilizing efforts. For example, if you need to make an appointment to take your car in for repairs, how long between realizing it and going the appointment does it take, three days, three months? Beyond setting a goal and taking action, what is it that changes things for you? Thoughts, actions, external influences and what are steps in that process?

Too often we think of something we want to change and when it doesn't happen as quickly as we'd like we get discouraged. Knowing your timing in the change process can help you press on and be encouraged that with effort and continued attention to the goal you can make it happen. If you can make it to work or a party, you can step up and accomplish what you want to accomplish.

Here are some other examples. Let's say that you've decided that every time you have a negative thought, you're going to use CBT and reframing or mindfulness to refocus your attention. If you've never practiced that before the first step is to identify when, what, and how you'll know to activate that action. It must involve what your brain is already used to doing which means to leverage an already existing process and its information. You must visualize when and where and see yourself doing it. If you practice that often enough in your mind first, it will serve as a placeholder for the mind to actually do it when the time comes. The brain remembers stuff by sensory, cognitive, emotive, and other physical stimuli. The more of those that you engage the stronger the neurological signal to establish and sustain the pattern both in thinking and behaving. Your feelings are the aftermath in that process. This means, don't be hard on yourself if _"at first you don't succeed, try, try again!"_ but make sure you have a solid plan with these variables at play.

Another example is if you want to quit smoking. You must first find a way to disrupt and destabilize the existing process. One way is to not allow yourself to smoke where and when you usually do. Delay gratification and only smoke in a specific isolated place while at the same time telling yourself that you don't like smoking versus engaging with feelings and thoughts of relief that you finally got a _"puff"_. You use the same process but change the content of perception. This can take days and weeks and is only the start to a longer process of change when it comes to addictions, but you get the picture. With small, calculated, and planned-out steps of intervention with yourself and with consistently successful effort to change your pattern the brain can become more alert rather than operating by automation. This is where you get an opportunity to gain control.

In terms of your own change process, consider the things you want to change and be more mindful of, what are they?

_____

_____

_____

_____

_____

_____

What have you tried before and what may need to change to start thinking about it in a different way?

_____

_____

_____

_____

_____

_____

What behavior or action would you need to target and disrupt?

_____

_____

_____

_____

_____

_____

To set up your process of change and understand where your "controls" are, do a simple test for a week by using a neutral habit you already engage in, like where you put your car keys when you walk in the door. Try putting them in a new spot consistently and see how long it takes you to get to a point of automation – *doing it without thinking*. How many times and what did you need to do to redirect yourself or remember what you were in the process of changing? Were there feelings or thoughts that got in the way? Make some notes to formulate the details that work for you to change this one simple behavior by being mindful (use the techniques and tools identified above as needed). How did it work?

_____

_____

_____

_____

_____

What was easy and what was hard? Is it something that can translate to other similar barriers that you run into with more important changes you've tried to make before?

_____

_____

_____

_____

_____

_____

_____

Were there tools that worked better than others and which time of the day was most effective for following through?

_____

_____

_____

_____

_____

How long did it take for you to change your behavior, putting the keys in a new place?

_____

_____

_____

_____

_____

What aspects of this process could you use to develop your own formula of action and expectation in terms of timelines for change in other areas of life that you wish to change?

_____

_____

_____

Chapter 13 ~
Set Up For Success

"There's no such thing as failure unless you give up.
Determination is key to success." ~ Dr. Vic

The end of the year seems to fly by. The holidays and observances can make it feel like a whirlwind by the time January 1st rolls around. It's a good time for reflection and putting things in perspective, especially if you have some New Year's resolutions in mind. For this month you'll simply take time to secure what you've learned about yourself in journaling throughout the year to capture the most important parts in a summary. This section can serve as your manual regarding YOU in the coming year. When you get off track, feel overwhelmed, or stressed, whether it's from going on vacation, starting a new job, daily demands, or facing difficult times that throw you off, instead of thinking you've backslidden or go back to believing you are *"depressed"* or *"anxious"*, remind yourself what makes life work for you. There is always something within your power that you can tap into if you know what to look for. You know some stuff about yourself now but remembering it all will require some ongoing awareness and evaluation. Setting yourself up for success in the coming year, can start right here. How?

The mind tends to reorganize information in its network when new experiences occur. It may also adapt or get desensitized towards information. This means that even when you do *"see"* or *"experience"* something useful, you may dismiss it. Likewise, the meaning may change over time. If something doesn't seem to hold the same weight as it did before you may want to sit with whatever you wrote a bit longer and meditate on it. What was happening in your life that made it meaningful? Why was it important to you? How did it help? Being successful has a lot to do with being mindful and not letting too many things cloud your life and mind. Likewise, there may be things you can cross-off when you've outgrown them. What you need, believe, or value at age 20 may not be the same at age 30, 40, or 70. Just because it doesn't make you feel the same now as it once did doesn't mean it can't be meaningful now. As you go through your notes to reflect on this year's journaling there are three things to consider:

1. Which rules and tools worked for you?
2. What things do you want to remember as positive triggers?
3. What do you need to feel your best and maintain your successes on a daily and weekly basis?

Copyright © 2021, V. Lännerholm, PsyD (ABD), LPCC, LPC, NCC

Rules & Tools

As you reflect on your overall experiences this year, what stands out? If you met some of your goals or found a tool that worked, how did you do it and how did it work? Think of it like setting up a game, how will you score a goal next year? What play will you need to set up on a daily or weekly basis? Unlike the negative messages and rules others put upon you through childhood or perhaps a bad relationship, if you were to write a rule-book to follow for yourself in life, what would it include? What are the boundaries you can't cross with yourself?

Maybe call it the "*Laws of Self-Care*". Here are some examples:

No bullying	Encourage
No judging	Support
No criticizing	Ask permission
Don't bring up stuff from the past	Read notes
Catch and release – let it go	Check
Observe	Call/reach out

As you review the life satisfaction categories you explored this year, keep this rule book in mind and add things of relevance as they pop up for those areas. When you needed strength in the past, what worked? If you need new ideas, then go back to what you wrote about yourself in that respective chapter. When you feel like nothing is working or boundaries are blurring, what are your red flags? What are your big rocks and are you prioritizing your values? Make a note of your thoughts from this year for easy reference in the next year.

Reminders

When stress comes it can be extremely difficult to stay on task, even to remember what your goals are and what's important in the moment. Feelings and emotions can blind and deceive you to make it seem like you don't really want what you want at times. You may second-guess and question rather than focus on what you can do. Reminders are critical when those times come in life, and they don't have to be philosophical or particularly profound. Everyday discoveries you made this year can be the key in pulling you back to a place of balance. The shorter and simpler the better.

Examples of reminders could be about who you are, what you believe, a quote, a faith-based or spiritual prayer or tradition, a kind word someone spoke over you, a saying, events that were difficult that made you strong where you overcame and survived, or anything else that resonates with you. Reminders should take you back to a place of comfort, strength, and grounding.

As the title of this book implies, the most important part of managing yourself is minding that inner dialogue. Reminders is a part of that work and you've done some great work in going through this book and facing some difficult questions. You can use all of that in the future to change your mindset or perspective and thus indirectly impact how you feel and what you do.

Some people develop *"pep-talks"* for themselves out of their journal notes by writing a paragraph to keep handy. Others use reminders meditatively at the end of difficult days to reconcile and let things go. Reminders don't have to be long; they just need to hold critical *cues* and values similar to those positive triggers you reviewed. Reminders should be clear to help your mind retrieve the whole of them and use them effectively in the moment when you see them. They can also serve as the foundation for setting new plans, goals, and imagine your life in a new way.

Reminders can be *"action"* items. For example, if one of your rules is to make sure you get to bed on time because you need a certain amount of sleep for self-care, then how are you going to make sure you don't snooze or shut off the reminder in your phone? Remember the brain is unfortunately really good at redirecting to what is *"easy"*. Training yourself to do and think something new will intention and continual effort until something can become automated. As you go through your journal notes in each topic area, keep in mind what you want to remember, and put it in as brief of a sentence in that section as possible. Then all you need to do is remember to look at your notes in the future.

Maintaining Your Gains

As you look through the past year of notes, how have you changed? What did you do and what was circumstantial? What remained the same? No matter what the progress is that you've made towards your hopes or goals some things have changed. Maybe you discovered that you aren't sure yet what you want to change or how it could work. Maybe your goal was to start journaling. Even if you wrote in only one or two chapters this year, you have made progress. Don't lose sight of the small gains and successes. The next year can serve to then maintain that and leverage what worked towards greater achievement this year. Life satisfaction must be your measure and not someone else's. You'll never be satisfied if you compare. Be honest in your review of your notes to document changes for the good or bad so that you can maintain and not go back. To step up for yourself and be encouraged.

Maintaining your successes and the investment you made this year in journaling can look different for everyone. Here are some things to consider when making some notes in each of the chapter domains below:

- ✓ How will you recognize when you are off track from a routine, goal, value, or need?
- ✓ How can you document cause and effects to quickly identify those slippery slopes and red flags?
- ✓ What are the points where you feel good – what should your aim be daily?
- ✓ What works for you to feel connected, grounded, and safe psychologically, emotionally, and physically?

Goals

Goals ~ Goal-setting and planning (what you want).

☐ _____

☐ _____

☐ _____

☐ _____

_____

_____

_____

_____

_____

Stressors

Stressors ~ Learn to mind your stressors (things that get in the way, vulnerabilities).

☐ _____

☐ _____

☐ _____

☐ _____

_____

_____

_____

_____

_____

Needs

Needs ~ Understanding and meeting your needs (your baseline).

☐ _____

☐ _____

☐ _____

☐ _____

_____
_____
_____
_____
_____

Values

Values ~ Learning about your values (what's important).

☐ _____

☐ _____

☐ _____

☐ _____

_____
_____
_____
_____
_____

Self-Care

Self-Care ~ Options for practicing self-care (balancing needs, stress, values, goals).

☐ _____

☐ _____

☐ _____

☐ _____

_____
_____

_____
_____
_____

Beliefs & Motivation

Beliefs & Motivation~ where resilience comes from (why you do what you do).

☐ _____

☐ _____

☐ _____

☐ _____

_____
_____
_____
_____
_____

Strengths

Strengths ~ Finding your strengths (what gives you control to feel powerful).

☐ _____

☐ _____

☐ _____

☐ _____

_____
_____
_____
_____
_____

Relationships

Relationships ~ Improving understanding relating (communication, others' needs/values).

☐ _____

☐ _____

☐ _____

☐ _____

_____
_____
_____
_____
_____

Boundaries

Boundaries ~ Allowing physical, emotional, and psychological space (yours/others).

☐ _____

☐ _____

☐ _____

☐ _____

_____
_____
_____
_____
_____

Patterns & Habits

Patterns & Habits~ Identifying patterns and habits (what works/what doesn't).

☐ _____

☐ _____

☐ _____

☐ _____

_____
_____
_____
_____
_____

Time

Time ~ Managing and prioritizing your time (reset and take charge).

☐ _____

☐ _____

☐ _____

☐ _____

_____
_____
_____
_____
_____

Mindfulness

Mindfulness ~Being present in the moment (while memories are being made).

☐ _____

☐ _____

☐ _____

☐ _____

_____
_____
_____
_____
_____

My Change Process

In each of these, make a note of what you have found success with before whether an example or specific steps you need to keep in mind as to how you engage in "change".

☐   Identify Target

_____
_____
_____
_____
_____

☐   Intervene with Tools/Techniques

_____
_____
_____
_____
_____

☐   Practice & Timeline Expectations

_____
_____
_____
_____
_____

Tools and Targets

In your attempts to make changes or maintain congruence, which tools and targets are most important for you to remember to try from week 3 and 4?

_____
_____
_____
_____
_____
_____
_____
_____
_____
_____

Resources

The next few pages can serve as a central place to capture resources that resonate with you over the year that you think would be helpful to revisit in the future. These can include links to websites, YouTube videos, names of people you follow, books etc.

☐ _____

☐ _____

☐ _____

☐ _____

☐ _____

☐ _____

☐ _____

☐ _____

☐ _____

☐ _____

☐ _____

☐ _____

☐ _____

☐ _____

☐ _____

☐ _____

☐ _____

☐ _____

☐ _____

☐ _____

☐ _____

☐ _____

☐ _____

☐ _____

☐ _____

☐ _____

☐ _____

☐ _____

☐ _____

☐ _____

☐ _____

☐ _____

☐ _____

☐ _____

☐ _____

☐ _____

☐ _____

☐ _____

☐ _____

- ☐ _____
- ☐ _____
- ☐ _____
- ☐ _____
- ☐ _____
- ☐ _____
- ☐ _____
- ☐ _____
- ☐ _____
- ☐ _____
- ☐ _____
- ☐ _____
- ☐ _____
- ☐ _____
- ☐ _____
- ☐ _____
- ☐ _____
- ☐ _____
- ☐ _____
- ☐ _____

Crisis & Emergency Information

Here is a list of common national resources that are available at no cost to you. You may want to paperclip this page for easy access later. Some of resources offer crisis intervention options. There is national legislation and plans to add a mental health emergency line by 2022, similar to dialing "9-1-1"[35]. There may also be local resources in your city or state. Most state *Health and Human Service or Department of Health agencies* has a list of resources. If you are covered under a health insurance plan, they often provide information on their website on what to do in case of an emergency and often offer referral services. Lastly, there may be a phone number on the back of your insurance card to call.

Aging and Disabled, Administration for Community Living
Independence, integration, and inclusion.
- https://acl.gov/

Bullying – what to do as a kid, teen, parent/adult
- https://www.stopbullying.gov/resources/get-help-now

Caregiver Resources
- https://www.hhs.gov/programs/providers-and-facilities/resources-for-caregivers/index.html

Domestic Violence – 1-800-799-7233 (SAFE), Text: 88788
(online chat available)
- https://www.thehotline.org/

Find a Therapist & Treatment Locator
- https://www.psychologytoday.com/us
- https://www.findtreatment.gov/

Helpline & Treatment Referral - 1-800-662-HELP (4357)
- https://www.samhsa.gov/find-help/national-helpline

Mental Health Resources
- https://www.nimh.nih.gov/health/
- https://www.mentalhealthfirstaid.org/
- https://screening.mhanational.org/screening-tools/
- https://www.samhsa.gov/public-messages

Native American Helpline - Strong Hearts 1-844-762-8483
(online chat available)
- https://strongheartshelpline.org/

Psychological First Aid – Disaster response

- https://www.apa.org/practice/programs/dmhi/psychological-first-aid

Suicide Crisis Hotline – 1-800-273-8255 (online chat available)

- https://suicidepreventionlifeline.org/talk-to-someone-now/

Veteran's Crisis Line - 1-800-273-8255 (online chat available)

- https://www.veteranscrisisline.net/
- https://www.ptsd.va.gov/PTSD/professional/treat/index.asp

Youth hotlines and resources – TXT 4 HELP, txt 839863, 1-800-852-8336

- http://nationalsafeplace.org/text-4-help/
- https://teenlineonline.org/talk-now/
- https://youth.gov/section/hotlines

Your Emergency Numbers and Contacts:

☐ _____
☐ _____
☐ _____
☐ _____
☐ _____
☐ _____
☐ _____
☐ _____
☐ _____
☐ _____
☐ _____
☐ _____
☐ _____
☐ _____
☐ _____
☐ _____
☐ _____
☐ _____
☐ _____
☐ _____
☐ _____

Acknowledgements

For my clients:
Thank you for sharing part of your journey with me.
You are my greatest teachers.

Footnotes

[1] Life Satisfaction Scale Domains

[2] Martin Seligman, Positive Psychology

[3] Substance Abuse and Mental Health Services Administration, https://mfpcc.samhsa.gov/ENewsArticles/Article12b_2017.aspx

[4] The Shining, 1980 starring Jack Nicholson.

[5] Placebo effect is an effect produced in a person when they attribute a treatment or medicine to have caused a change in their condition (feelings or otherwise) even when it had no properties or capacity to do so.

[6] National Alliance on Mental Illness – https://www.nami.org

[7] Questions adapted from the Boundaries Screen, 1999, by www.Dr-Jane-Bolton.com.

[8] The Mere Exposure Effect is the brain-child of Robert Zajonc around 1968 and his work at the University of Michigan.

[9] The concept of Paired Association is attributed to learning studies conducted by Mary Whiton Calkins work in 1894.

[10] Classical Conditioning was a concept established by Ivan P. Pavlov, a Russian Psychologist, in the 1897.

[11] Schemas are knowledge structures about a concept, idea, people, self, the world, that endures and serves as a guide to perception, interpretation, imagination, and problem solving. American Psychological Association, 2007.

[12] State-dependent learning is a phenomenon where the brain's memory is able to recall information much easier when it is in the same physical and mental state as the time when it learned something.

[13] The concept of Fundamental Attribution Error is most often credited to Lee Ross in 1977.

[14] The concept of "biases" is credited to various work in cognitive psychology by Paul Slovic, Daniel Kahneman, and Amos Tversky crossing the 1970's and 1980s.

[15] Adapted from McCormick, 1971, and the Life Script by Dr. Wells, Counseling & Psychotherapy Institute, NM.

[16] Cozolino, 2010.

[17] "Conditioning" is a process by which something is "trained" or "manipulated" into a state of being or doing. Like taking a piece of hard leather and stripping it by cleaning then drying it and rubbing in layers of oil at regular intervals which eventually creates a soft and pliable state that you can mold around anything

or sew to your liking. Psychological conditioning then molds the mind and behavioral responses to react in a certain way with certain stimuli.

[18] *Differentiation of self* is a process whereby a person is able to distinguish thoughts from emotions and maintain personal perspective and agency in terms of feelings, goals, opinions, and identity in the face of external pressures to the contrary. Usually addressed in Murray Bowens Family Systems Theory.

[19] Metacognition credited to John Flavell 1970s based on "Metamemory".

[20] Reeve, M. 2009.

[21] Congruence/incongruence: Rogers, C., 1977.

[22] Cruwys & Gunaseelan, 2016; Henderson et al., 2007; Orbell, S., & Henderson, C. (2016). Automatic effects of illness schema activation on behavioral manifestations of illness health. APA; Oris et al., 2016, 2018;

[23] Merton, R. K., 1948 "self-fulfilling prophecy" concept.

[24] Choudhry, et al., 2016; Rickwood et al., 2007; Stunden et al., 2020; Velasco et al., 2020.

[25] 5/7 Rule was developed by Vicki Lännerholm (aka Dr. Vic) during her PsyD dissertation project 2019 based on a study by.

[26] 75/25 Model of Effort was developed by Vicki Lännerholm (aka Dr. Vic) while working with clients in counseling during the year 2020 to redefine goal parameters based on the insurance model of 80/20 coverage and that nothing is perfect.

[27] The origins of RUOK ALEC are a bit unclear but appear to be as recent as 2017 with an Australian campaign according to research conducted by Ross & Bassilios in 2019.

[28] ALGEE is a part of Mental Health First Aid training as a quick way to remember how to assess risk when someone is in distress. It is also their "mascot".

[29] REBT (Rational Emotive Behavior Therapy) was developed by Albert Ellis in 1955 and represents an action plan to address cognitive and behavioral components of a person's emotional experience.

[30] The origins of F.O.C.U.S and S.T.O.P. are unclear but appear to be original ideas based on work by Jon Kabat-Zinn.

[31] H.A.L.T. has its roots in 12-step recovery programs for addiction and substance use issues to quicky differentiate between cravings and basic physical needs and thus take action to meet needs rather than turn to the substance or other type of habit.

[32] The Opt-Out is a communication boundary tool developed by Vicki Lännerholm (aka Dr. Vic) as a part of her Buffer Zone Model of Interpersonal Dialogue.

[33] The RESPECTFUL model of counseling was developed by D'Andrea and Daniels in 2005.

[34] The W.I.N. principle appears to have its roots in football, specifically as a tool that Lou Holtz used in his coaching strategies with players at the University of Notre Dame (Dave Johnson PhD, LMFT, 2018).

35 https://www.npr.org/sections/health-shots/2020/10/19/925447354/new-law-creates-988-hotline-for-mental-health-emergencies